Environmental Assessment of the Gaza Strip

following the escalation of hostilities in
December 2008 – January 2009

United Nations Environment Programme

Table of contents

Foreword   3

Acronyms and abbreviations   4

Weights and measures   5

1. Background   6

2. Environmental assessment of the Gaza Strip   11

   2.1 Introduction 11

   2.2 Scope of the environmental assessment 12

   2.3 Environmental assessment methodology 13

   2.4 Background research 15

   2.5 Remote sensing analysis..16

   2.6 Field work..18

   2.7 Laboratory analysis 26

   2.8 Limitations and constraints..26

3. Results and discussions   27

   3.1 Introduction 27

   3.2 Damages directly attributable to the recent escalation of violence 27

   3.3 Environmental issues pre-dating the recent escalation of hostilities that were aggravated by it 38

   3.4 Institutional assessment...68

4. Recommendations   69

   4.1 Introduction 69

   4.2 Recommendations for the restoration of damage
       caused by the recent escalation of hostilities..70

   4.3 Recommendations for the remediation of pre-existing environmental
       degradation that was exacerbated by the recent hostilities 70

5. Economic assessment   72

   5.1 Introduction 72

   5.2 Scope of the economic assessment...72

   5.3 Economic assessment methodology 73

   5.4 Limitations and constraints..74

   5.5 Findings...75

Endnotes   85

Appendix I: UNEP Governing Council Decision 25/12:
               The environmental situation in the Gaza Strip...................................87

Appendix II: List of assessments conducted in the Gaza Strip
               after the recent escalation of violence and hostilities.......................88

Appendix III: References...90

Appendix IV: Bibliography..92

Appendix V: List of contributors...96

Foreword

This report and its findings are based on field work by a team of international experts deployed by UNEP following its Governing Council's Decision 25/12 in February 2009, requesting UNEP to assess the environmental damage and carry out an economic evaluation of the rehabilitation and restoration of the environment in the Gaza Strip following the escalation of hostilities in December 2008 and late January 2009.

As part of this process, I personally travelled to the region in April 2009, and met with senior Palestinian and Israeli representatives. I also had the opportunity to visit various sites, including parts of the Gaza Strip.

The team of experts, coordinated by UNEP's Post-Conflict and Disaster Management Branch (PCDMB), concludes that a wide range of environmental challenges require urgent resolve.

These range from safe disposal of large amounts of rubble, some of which is contaminated with substances like asbestos, to sewage pollution of coastal waters. Some of the challenges have been aggravated by recent events but their roots pre-date the latest hostilities.

The most urgent and challenging finding is the state of the underground water supplies, upon which the Palestinian people – and to a large extent the people of Israel – rely for drinking and agricultural irrigation water.

Years of over-abstraction and pollution now mean that the sustainability of the Gaza Strip is now in serious doubt unless the aquifer is 'rested' and solutions such as improved sanitation and desalination are introduced.

This report outlines a range of economically costed options for managing the current situation and leading the Gaza Strip onto a sustainable path.

It is hoped that the facts and economic analysis presented here can assist and guide the relevant national and local authorities and the inter-national community to design forward-looking recovery strategies and transformative investment decisions.

This report, which has been submitted to the UN Secretary-General Ban Ki-Moon, is the latest post-conflict environmental assessment undertaken by UNEP. Others include those carried out in the Balkans, Iraq, Liberia, Afghanistan and Sudan.

As in previous studies, UNEP's report on the Gaza Strip could not have been possible without the support of a wide range of UN agencies operating in the region.

I would thus like to thank colleagues including UNSCO, UNRWA, UNDP, OCHA, WHO, UNDSS and UNMAS. UNEP stands ready to work with the UN family and relevant authorities in the region in forging a more sustainable and peaceful future for the people of this region.

Achim Steiner
United Nations Under-Secretary General
Executive Director
of the United Nations Environment Programme

Acronyms and abbreviations

BOD	biological oxygen demand
BTEX	benzene, toluene, ethyl benzene and xylene
CAMP	Coastal Aquifer Management Plan
CAPEX	capital expenditure
CMWU	Coastal Municipalities Water Utility
COD	chemical oxygen demand
DDD	dichlorodiphenyldichloroethane
DDE	dichlorodiphenyldichloroethylene
DDT	dichlorodiphenyltrichloroethane
EPA	Environmental Protection Agency
EQA	Environmental Quality Authority
EWC	European Waste Catalogue
FAO	Food and Agriculture Organization
GPS	Global Positioning System
GSSO	German Sewage Sludge Ordnance
HHCW	hazardous healthcare waste
IDF	Israeli Defence Forces
LAGA	Laender-Arbeitsgemeinschaft Abfall (German Federal States' Working Group on Waste)
NGO	non-governmental organization
OCHA	Office for the Coordination of Humanitarian Affairs
OPEX	operational expenditure
PAH	polynuclear aromatic hydrocarbon
PAPP	Programme of Assistance to the Palestinian People
PCB	polychlorinated biphenyl
PCEA	post-conflict environmental assessment
PCM	phase contrast microscopy
PWA	Palestinian Water Authority
SPCSO	soil protection and contaminated sites ordinance
TPH	total petroleum hydrocarbon
UK	United Kingdom
UN	United Nations
UNDP	United Nations Development Programme
UNDSS	United Nations Department of Safety and Security
UNEP	United Nations Environment Programme
UNICEF	United Nations Children's Fund
UNITAR	United Nations Institute for Training and Research
UNMAS	United Nations Mine Action Service
UNOSAT	United Nations Operational Satellite Applications Programme
UNRWA	United Nations Relief and Works Agency
USD	United States dollar
UXO	unexploded ordnance
VOC	volatile organic compound
WHO	World Health Organization

Weights and measures

cfu	colony forming unit
cm	centimetre
cm3	cubic centimetre
ft	foot
kg	kilogramme
km	kilometre
l	litre
m2	square metre
m3	cubic metre
mg	milligramme
ml	millilitre
mm	millimetre
m/s	metre/second
ng	nanogramme
µg	microgramme
µm	micrometre
µs	microsiemens

1 Background

The Gaza Strip has been a theatre of conflict for decades. Each of these conflicts has left its mark, and over time, a significant environmental footprint has developed in the Gaza Strip. During the most recent fighting – between 27 December 2008 and 18 January 2009 – Israeli Defence Forces (IDF) conducted a major combined military operation in the Gaza Strip. The operation comprised bombardment by land, sea and air, and incursions into the Gaza Strip by Israeli troops. Before and during that period, Hamas and other Palestinian militant groups fired rockets from Gaza into Israel and engaged Israeli troops in Gaza during the ground invasion.

The fighting resulted in extensive casualties and the destruction of homes, livelihoods and infrastructure. With fighting taking place in densely populated areas, and with hospitals and UN facilities being hit by shells, there was almost no safe space in the Gaza Strip. As the borders were sealed, civilians had no place to flee, and bore the brunt of the fighting.

Homes and public infrastructure throughout the Gaza Strip sustained extensive damage. Gaza City was the worst hit. A unilateral Israeli ceasefire on 18 January, followed a day later by a unilateral ceasefire by Hamas and other Palestinian factions, put an end to the fighting.

The Israeli army completed its withdrawal from the Gaza Strip on 21 January.

The environmental situation in the Gaza Strip was already serious prior to these events, due to underinvestment in environmental systems, lack of progress on priority environmental projects and the collapse of governance mechanisms. The recent escalation of hostilities caused additional damage and increased the pressure on environmental facilities and institutions. Two of the most striking examples are the significant volume of demolition debris that was generated and the serious damage done to the sewage system. Other adverse environmental impacts include the widespread destruction of agricultural areas, damage to smaller industrial enterprises and an increase in pollution discharged into the Mediterranean and into the groundwater.

According to a United Nations (UN) damage assessment carried out using satellite imagery, 2,692 buildings and 180 greenhouses were destroyed or severely damaged during the hostilities and 167 kilometres of road were damaged. The assessment revealed 220 impact craters on roads and bridges and more than 700 craters on open or agricultural land. Utilities infrastructure in energy (fuel and electricity), transportation and telecommunications also sustained severe damage during the crisis. Water supplies were affected by damage to water wells and drinking water pipes, as were wastewater systems.

Box 1.   The Gaza Strip: geography, climate and population

The Gaza Strip is a narrow strip of land on the Mediterranean coast. It borders Israel to the east and north and Egypt to the south. It is approximately 41 kilometres long, and between 6 and 12 kilometres wide, with a total area of 378 square kilometres.

The Gaza Strip has a temperate climate, with mild winters and dry, hot summers subject to drought. Average rainfall is about 300 mm. The terrain is flat or rolling, with dunes near the coast. The highest point is Abu 'Awdah (Joz Abu 'Auda), at 105 metres above sea level. There are no permanent water bodies in the Gaza Strip, though large-scale sewage ponds and sewage flowing through Wadi Gaza have become de facto hydraulic features.

In 1948, the Gaza Strip had a population of less than 100,000 people. By 2007, approximately 1.4 million Palestinians lived in the Gaza Strip, of whom almost one million were UN-registered refugees. The current population is estimated to be in excess of 1.5 million, distributed across five Governorates. Gaza City, which is the biggest governorate, has about 400,000 inhabitants. The two other main governorates are Khan Younis (population 200,000) in central Gaza, and Rafah (population 150,000) to the south. The majority of people live in refugee camps.

Map 1.   Regional map

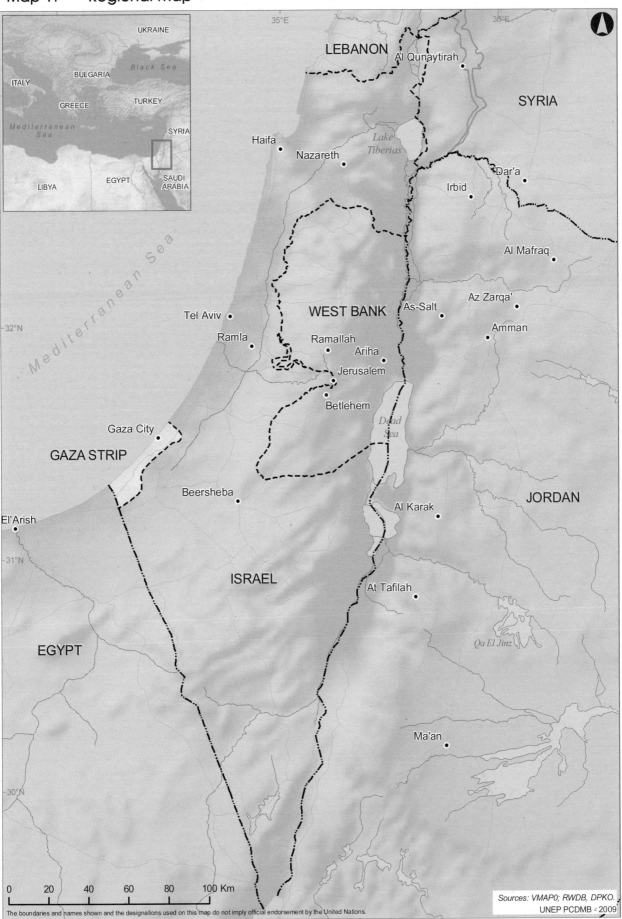

Sources: VMAP0; RWDB, DPKO.
UNEP PCDMB - 2009

Environmental Assessment of the Gaza Strip

Map 2.   Gaza Strip

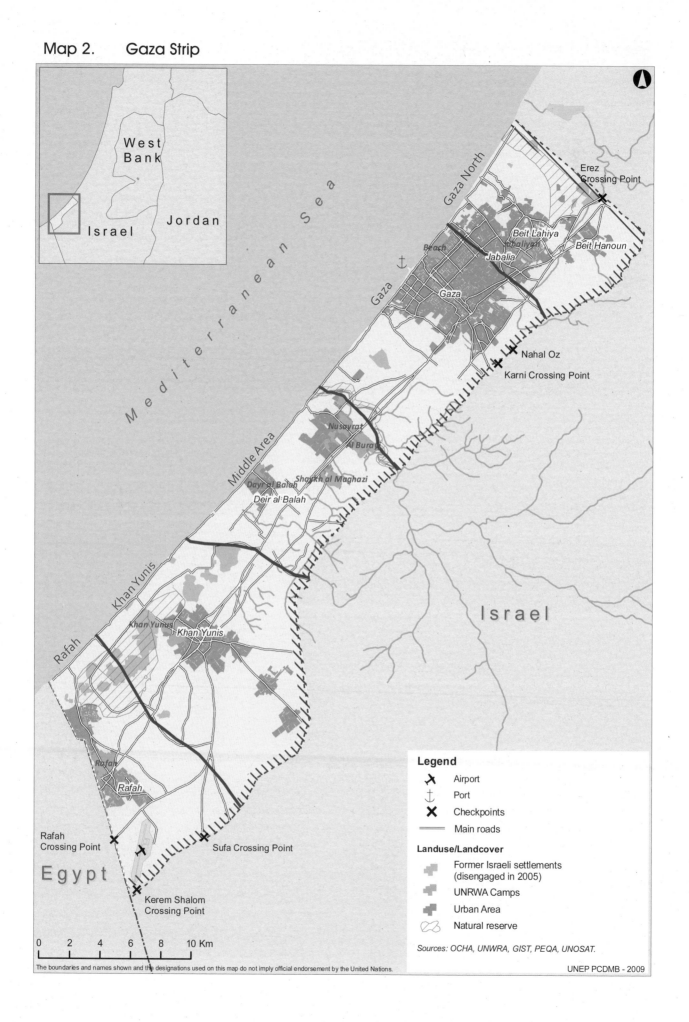

Legend

✈ Airport

⊥ Port

✖ Checkpoints

── Main roads

Landuse/Landcover

▦ Former Israeli settlements (disengaged in 2005)

▦ UNRWA Camps

▦ Urban Area

◠ Natural reserve

Sources: OCHA, UNWRA, GIST, PEQA, UNOSAT.

The boundaries and names shown and the designations used on this map do not imply official endorsement by the United Nations.

UNEP PCDMB - 2009

UNEP expert in the Gaza Strip during the UN Early Recovery Assessment mission in January 2009

The United Nations Environment Programme (UNEP) has many years of experience working in the region. As soon as the recent escalation of hostilities began in the Gaza Strip, UNEP started to track developments and to study their implication for the environment. In late January 2009, within ten days of the ceasefire and upon request from the Palestinian Environmental Quality Authority (EQA), a UNEP staff member was deployed to the Gaza Strip to assess and report on the environmental impacts of the hostilities.

In February 2009, the UNEP Governing Council discussed the situation in the Gaza Strip at its 25th session held in Nairobi. Expressing its deep concern at the negative implications of the environmental impacts on the Gaza Strip caused by the escalation of violence between December 2008 and January 2009, it requested the UNEP Executive Director to immediately deploy a mission of environmental experts to the Gaza Strip, in coordination with other relevant international organizations, to: (i) assess the environmental impacts on the Gaza Strip caused by the escalation of violence in late 2008; (ii) carry out an economic evaluation of the rehabilitation and restoration of the environmental damage; and (iii) report the findings to the Secretary-General of the United Nations (see Appendix I).

UNEP's Executive Director accordingly travelled to the region in April 2009. During this visit, the Executive Director had extensive discussions with both Palestinian and Israeli decision-makers, and finalized the terms of reference and arrangements for the technical environmental assessment mission that was to follow. The Executive Director also met with the key UN agencies active in the region. The Government of Israel agreed to facilitate the assessment, and various UN agencies promised full logistical support to the mission.

In May 2009, the UNEP technical mission, consisting of eight international experts, travelled to the Gaza Strip with equipment and sampling kits. The United Nations Development Programme/Programme of Assistance to the Palestinian People (UNDP/PAPP) in Jerusalem and the Gaza Strip provided logistical support for the mission. The UNEP team received a thorough briefing on unexploded ordnance (UXO) in the impacted area from the United Nations Mine Action Service (UNMAS) and a general security briefing from the United Nations Department of Safety and Security (UNDSS). UNDP officials involved in various aspects of assessment and restoration (housing, agriculture, health, etc.) joined the UNEP team to act as local guides and facilitate the field mission.

The UNEP team spent the first three days conducting meetings with UN colleagues and other local stakeholders, as well as conducting reconnaissance visits to all the clusters of impacted sites, which had been identified from satellite image analysis. This was followed by a comprehensive field visit, using sampling and measuring equipment. During the course of this detailed visit, the team visited 35 individual locations or clusters of impacted areas, ranging from bombed-out houses to industrial units destroyed by ground action. The team took samples and photographs, and conducted ad hoc interviews with people in the impacted areas who had been affected by the recent hostilities.

Samples were taken in triplicate and shipped from the Gaza Strip to Jerusalem. The purpose of triplicate samples was to enable the Palestinian and Israeli authorities to carry out their own analysis in addition to UNEP's. One set of samples was provided to the Palestinian Authority, together with the analysis matrix (a table showing which samples would be analysed for which chemical parameters). A second set of samples, with the analysis matrix, was provided to the Government of Israel. The third set of samples was shipped to Europe for analysis at independent laboratories contracted by UNEP.

In addition to background research and field work, satellite image analysis was an important component of the UNEP assessment, as the locations for initial reconnaissance were chosen mainly from targets identified from satellite images. The field observations and geo-coordinated photographs were then used to finalize the satellite image analysis.

The Governing Council decision also expressly requested UNEP to carry out an economic evaluation of the rehabilitation and restoration of the environmental damage in the Gaza Strip. Accordingly, an environmental economist joined the mission to gather relevant information, such as costing of the various physical resources (e.g. land, water supplies) and services (e.g. labour, healthcare). Baseline information about employment and the health situation in the area was also collected.

Generally speaking, the environmental issues observed by UNEP in the Gaza Strip could be classified into three categories: (a) direct environmental impacts of the December 2008-January 2009 hostilities; (b) environmental degradation that existed prior to the recent events but was exacerbated by them; and (c) environmental issues that were not caused or aggravated by the recent escalation of hostilities.

Damaged building in the Gaza Strip

In this assessment, only the first two categories – environmental damage that was caused or exacerbated by the recent escalation of hostilities – were studied. Environmental issues like the impacts of climate change or desertification, which are also significant problems in the Gaza strip but were neither caused nor aggravated by the recent events, were not examined as they clearly fell outside the assessment mandate. Also excluded, for reasons of methodological limitation, were obvious environmental impacts of the escalation of hostilities that were no longer observable, such as air pollution from burning buildings, for example.

This report presents the initial action undertaken by UNEP immediately following the cessation of hostilities in the Gaza Strip in January 2009, and summarizes the scientific findings of the complex assessment process carried out by UNEP at the request of its Governing Council during the spring and early summer of 2009. Concrete recommendations are provided for the remediation of environmental damage caused by the recent escalation of hostilities, as well as for longer-term improvement of the environmental situation in the Gaza Strip.

2 Environmental assessment of the Gaza Strip

2.1 Introduction

Post-conflict environmental assessments (PCEAs) are scientific studies of the environmental situation in a given location following a conflict. They do not seek to apportion blame, but rather to examine the development of environmental issues in the context of the conflict and to chart a way forward that promotes restoration of the impacted environment. Environmental assessments of this kind have two main purposes. First, they provide information and guidance to communities about the environmental risks to their lives or livelihoods arising from the conflict. Second, they inform other stakeholders (for example, governments and donors) about environmental priorities for post-conflict recovery and reconstruction.

While this assessment of the environmental and economic impacts on the Gaza Strip was requested by the Palestinian Authority, the mandate arose from a unanimous decision taken at the Governing Council of UNEP in February 2009. The mandate restricted the scope of the assessment to the impacts of the escalation of violence at the end of 2008 and in early 2009. As a result, this is a study of the environmental impacts of a specific event in a limited period of time, not a general assessment of the state of the environment in the Gaza Strip, or an analysis of the effects of other events in the region.

PCEAs typically start with a scoping mission by an environmental expert to the impacted area, which seeks to: (1) understand the geographic and technical scope of the environment affected by the conflict – this involves discussions with local experts, collection of background information and maps and reconnaissance visits to some affected sites; (2) to identify and engage local stakeholders who could assist with the study; and (3) to consider the logistics of project implementation, including any security issues.

In the context of this assessment, information was first gathered during a four-day mission by UNEP to the area in late January 2009, to identify environmental issues that might pose an immediate threat to human life. Working under the auspices of the UN Early Recovery Assessment mission, an expert visited sites where there had been widespread destruction of buildings and damage to the sewage system. Following the Governing Council decision, UNEP dispatched another staff member to the Gaza Strip in April 2009 to discuss the terms of reference of the assessment mission with stakeholders in the region, and to make all necessary logistical arrangements.

UNEP team in the Gaza Strip, May 2009

2.2 Scope of the environmental assessment

The scope of the assessment work included the following areas:

Solid waste management: The Israeli Defence Forces' (IDF) campaign in the Gaza Strip generated large quantities of solid waste, resulting primarily from the destruction of buildings. This kind of waste – rubble and other building materials – is often contaminated with hazardous materials, in particular asbestos. Even before the events of December 2008-January 2009, waste in the Gaza Strip was not segregated and disposed of in a systematic way, largely because of the deteriorating economic situation. Consequently, the creation of such large quantities of solid waste within such a short period of time overloaded the already inadequate infrastructure. The following issues were identified as priorities for the study:

- assess the volume and types of solid waste found in the Gaza Strip as a consequence of the escalation of hostilities;

- review the existing solid waste management infrastructure, including equipment, vehicles and final disposal sites, and its ability to absorb the additional waste;

- determine the extent to which regular waste and waste rubble were contaminated by hazardous materials such as hydrocarbons, chemical and hazardous healthcare waste, and the possibility for the segregation and safe disposal of these types of waste;

- assess the situation relating to the management of hazardous healthcare waste (HHCW);

- identify the opportunities to reuse and recycle some of the waste products, particularly building rubble;

- identify opportunities to create employment through the management of solid waste; and

- assess the economic cost of solid waste management (clearing, sorting, transporting, and recycling the waste, and disposing of any waste that cannot be reused).

Wastewater management: The most significant issue relating to wastewater management is the collection, storage, treatment and disposal of sewage. Not only did the Gaza Strip not have an adequate sewage system before the escalation of hostilities, but the existing infrastructure was impacted, including the main sewage treatment plant. Damaged treatment ponds released vast quantities of untreated sewage into the environment, further aggravating an already serious public health situation. Key priorities for this study were to:

- assess the state of the system for the collection, storage, treatment and disposal of sewage in the Gaza Strip;

- investigate how the existing infrastructure was affected by the escalation of violence, and identify urgent measures that may be needed to minimize the risk to public health;

- identify additional infrastructure needed to adequately manage wastewater issues in the Gaza Strip;

- identify opportunities to reuse wastewater (particularly important, given the scarcity of water within the Gaza Strip); and

- calculate the economic cost of the destruction of wastewater management infrastructure, including the additional public health impact on the community.

Management of contaminated land: During UNEP's visit to the Gaza Strip immediately after the ceasefire, it was observed that a number of small-scale enterprises, such as factories, cement plants and garages, had been damaged or destroyed during the hostilities. This inferred that numerous sites within the urban environment as well as on agricultural land were potentially contaminated. In addition, the recent fighting had involved the use of various kinds of ammunition that may have left traces in the impacted areas, potentially contaminating the land. Therefore the key priorities were to:

- identify the number and types of locations that could be classified as potentially contaminated sites;

- assess the degree of contamination and the various chemicals involved, including any possible contamination of water sources;

- provide recommendations for the isolation and containment of the areas;

- propose plans for the clean-up and, where necessary, remediation of contaminated sites, including the cost of clean-up; and

- calculate the total economic cost of land contamination, including the opportunity cost of taking contaminated land out of profitable use until it is cleaned up.

Institutional assessment: The international community, including UNEP, has in the past provided assistance to the Palestinian Environmental Quality Authority (EQA) and other ministries in the form of equipment and training for environmental measurement and information management in the Gaza Strip. It was important to evaluate the equipment and systems currently in operation, as the timely provision of reliable environmental information is crucial to making decisions about environmental matters. The priorities in this area were to:

- understand what systems were in place to monitor the environment in the Gaza Strip prior to the escalation of hostilities in December 2008 and January 2009;

- assess the current status of the monitoring equipment and systems in place in the Gaza Strip; and

- determine what equipment and support are needed to re-establish environmental monitoring and information management systems to the appropriate level.

Economic assessment: Once the extent of the physical damage to the environment had been assessed, and the measures required for rehabilitation had been identified, it was possible to calculate the total economic cost of the damage resulting from the escalation of violence in December 2008 and January 2009. The key elements of the calculation were:

- cost of restoring the environmental and public health infrastructure damaged as a result of the recent fighting;

- additional cost of handling, transporting and disposing of the solid waste generated during the hostilities, minus any revenue generated from the recycling of construction materials;

- cost of clean-up and remediation of the contaminated land, plus the opportunity cost of taking land out of profitable use in the interim;

- cost of re-establishing environmental measurement and information management systems that collapsed due to the recent hostilities and the ongoing blockade of goods and materials entering the Gaza Strip; and

- economic valuation of the loss and remediation of any recreational areas (such as beaches) that may have been contaminated by raw sewage, solid waste or hazardous materials released to the environment during the recent hostilities.

2.3   Environmental assessment methodology

UNEP post-conflict environmental assessments (PCEAs)

While UNEP has been conducting post-conflict environmental assessments (PCEAs) for over ten years, undertaking such a study is always methodologically challenging. For example, pre-existing baseline data is rarely available for an area emerging from conflict. In addition, logistics and security constraints in a post-conflict situation often limit the amount of time available for field work, as well as the size of the assessment team itself. Finally, PCEAs are usually conducted in a highly politicized context, and are therefore closely scrutinized by parties who may have diverging views on the causes and consequences of the hostilities. PCEAs thus require a scientifically robust methodology, as well as an independent and objective team. This need for methodological rigour, however, is often in direct tension with the limitations on time and logistics imposed by the post-conflict situation.

To meet these specific challenges, the following steps are taken. First and foremost, extensive background research is conducted prior to designing the scope and identifying the assessment team. This research is complemented with the detailed analysis of high-resolution satellite images, which are used for three main purposes: for creating detailed field maps; for identifying sites of interest for the field work; and, through time series analyses, for providing evidence of temporally isolated conflict-related impacts.

Second, to make optimal use of the experts' time in the field, reconnaissance visits are conducted to a large number of sites to select more relevant areas for detailed inspection. Locations visited in this first phase are selected from satellite image analysis, news reports (areas where major fighting took place, for example), and discussion with local officials and communities, as well as with other UN agencies. The reconnaissance visits are conducted using a structured checklist to ensure that the final selection of sites is made in an objective manner.

Third, due to logistics and time constraints, the number of areas that can be assessed in detail and the number of samples that can be collected at each of the sites need to be decided carefully. In this respect, UNEP's guiding principle is to ensure that all major impacted sites are visited, along with a representative number of typical sites. For example, if two major industries and a series of petrol stations are impacted during a conflict, both the industries and a sample of petrol stations will be selected for detailed assessment.

Fourth, the collection and laboratory analysis of field samples is a key feature of PCEAs. While many other environmental assessments are chiefly based on visual observation by technical experts, PCEAs gather as many samples as possible to complement field observations with objective scientific evidence. When needed, moreover, samples can be collected in duplicate or triplicate, and shared with the various parties to the conflict so that they can independently verify the work. The analysis of samples taken by UNEP is always conducted by independent international laboratories that have the required accreditation (ISO 17025 or equivalent).

The UNEP Governing Council decision requested an assessment of the "natural and environmental impacts [...] caused by the escalation of violence," and not a general study of all the destruction and damage that ensued from the hostilities. Evaluating the degree to which the environment has been impacted, however, can be challenging. There is no universally agreed standard for environmental quality, so that multiple standards prevail in most sectors. UNEP generally employs the most widely used international standards or guidelines for comparison, including the WHO guidelines for drinking water quality, and the Dutch Standards for soil contamination. When required, other national, regional or international standards are used.

Finally, the interest of the environment is best served when credible scientific evidence of the state of the environment and viable technical proposals

for rehabilitation are presented in a non-partisan manner. UNEP therefore systematically shares the terms of reference with the parties concerned, briefs the parties prior to and after the field work, shares samples and laboratory analysis protocols, and when possible shares the final draft of the PCEA report with the parties for a round of consultations, with a view to avoiding factual errors. While the assessment findings and recommendations remain strictly independent and objective, such transparent engagement of the parties works to build confidence in the PCEA's credibility. This has in turn facilitated support from both parties in implementing the recommendations. In addition, PCEA reports are reviewed by independent international experts to guarantee their scientific soundness and credibility.

Assessment of the Gaza Strip

In the case of the Gaza Strip, the standard methodology presented above required some adaptation. Indeed, two aspects of the Governing Council decision posed serious challenges to the UNEP technical team.

First, the decision restricted the analysis to the period of the recent escalation of hostilities, from 27 December 2008 to 18 January 2009. This entailed that obtaining a snapshot of the post-conflict environmental situation would not suffice. The observed environmental impacts would have to be related specifically to the recent events. This was further complicated by the fact that pre-conflict (before December 2008) data was not available. The UNEP team decided on an approach whereby the current environmental situation in the Gaza Strip would be classified into four separate categories.

a) Environmental impacts that were visible and measurable at the time of the assessment, and could be demonstrated to be directly linked to the recent escalation of hostilities. This included issues such as the vast quantities of demolition rubble, the destruction of orchards, and damage to water supply and sewage networks:

b) Environmental degradation that could be scientifically demonstrated to have been exacerbated by the hostilities, although the observed damage could not be entirely imputed to the recent events. This included issues such as groundwater pollution, sewage contamination and impacts on landfills;

c) Environmental issues that warranted attention but were neither caused by, nor aggravated by the recent hostilities, such as desertification and the environmental impacts of climate change linked; and

d) Environmental damage that must have occurred during the escalation of hostilities, but whose effects were no longer observable, such as air pollution resulting from the numerous fires burning in the Gaza Strip during the fighting.

In keeping with the Governing Council mandate, the UNEP team focused only on the first two categories. Sections 2.4 through 2.8 below detail the steps that were taken as part of the PCEA in the Gaza Strip.

Second, UNEP was requested to carry out an economic evaluation of the rehabilitation and restoration of the environmental damage in the Gaza Strip. While economic evaluation of environmental damages is a well established branch of economics, and specific economic evaluations of conflict-related impacts have been attempted in the past (after the 1991 Gulf War and after the 2006 conflict in Lebanon, for example), this presented UNEP with two methodological challenges.

The first and most fundamental was that standard evaluations pre-suppose a functioning market. The Gaza Strip, however, is essentially an aid economy in which 50 percent of the workforce is unemployed and up to 85 percent of the population depends on food aid of some kind. In this situation, very few normal goods and services have market-determined economic value. Calculating the economic value of environmental goods and services (e.g. groundwater quality, clean beaches) that are usually considered non-market goods in a non-functioning market was a challenge in itself.

When observed environmental damages were directly attributable to the recent events, engineering estimates from UN agencies that have experience in undertaking restoration projects were used as the basis of costing the restoration. When UN engineering estimates were not available, costing could in some cases be based on locally collected data. In instances where observed impacts were attributable to the recent hostilities, but no estimate could be calculated due to absence of data or methodological limitations, no costing was attempted.

In addition it should be noted that the direct costs of the observed damage were not considered as environmental costs: if a house was destroyed, for example, the cost of rebuilding it was considered a direct cost of the damage; the cost of handling the rubble and cleaning the site prior to rebuilding the house, however, was included as an environmental cost.

The second methodological challenge was that costing had to be done for the restoration of the environment in the Gaza Strip, including sectors in which environmental degradation had been aggravated by the recent hostilities, but was not fully imputable to them. It made neither economic nor environmental sense to calculate the cost of rehabilitating a damaged environmental sector to its pre-December 2008 state, as that state was unacceptable by international standards. In this specific instance, UNEP used engineering estimates to quantify the cost of restoration but made no attempt to attribute any percentage of the cost to the recent escalation of hostilities.

The detailed methodology of the economic assessment is presented in Chapter 5.

2.4   Background research

The prevailing security situation in the Gaza Strip presents many challenges for field work. UNDSS strictly limits the number of international UN personnel that can be in the Gaza Strip at any given time and restricts their movement. The IDF also limit the movement of people to and from the Gaza Strip. These restrictions make it essential to carry out as much preparatory work as possible, so that the field work can be minimized and targeted at the areas where it is most useful.

UNEP used reports prepared by other agencies – such as the United Nations Development Programme (UNDP), the World Health Organization (WHO), the United Nations Relief and Works Agency (UNRWA) – on infrastructural damage, and satellite image assessments undertaken by the United Nations Operational Satellite Applications Programme (UNOSAT), as the starting point for planning the field work.

It was clear from this early research that a large number of locations had been affected by the hostilities of December 2008-January 2009 (see Map 3) and that it would not be possible to visit every site. The UNEP experts who were to be deployed to the Gaza Strip met in Geneva in April 2009 and discussed the field work programme. It was agreed that the team would focus on two types of areas. The first was areas where environmental impacts were expected to be most severe. These were identified as industrial units, landfills, sewage treatment plants, sewage outfalls, water supply wells and impacted areas of the coastline. The second type was areas with widespread issues such as asbestos, drinking water quality and demolition debris. It was agreed that these areas would be sampled selectively.

The field work was then organized into three parts: (i) reconnaissance; (ii) detailed assessment of sites; and (iii) economic and institutional assessment (office-based interviews in the Gaza Strip and data gathering).

2.5   Remote sensing analysis

To prepare and support the team working in the field, UNEP obtained as much information as possible about sites of interest prior to the mission, including the location of impacted areas (e.g. industrial sites, water supply systems, nature reserves, cultivated land and residential areas); and damage to infrastructure (e.g. roads, bridges).

On the basis of this preliminary information, a set of maps was prepared to help experts navigate efficiently and safely between sites in the Gaza Strip, as well as within the sites themselves.

Table 1.   Details of satellite images used

Pre-crisis imagery used	Post-crisis imagery used
June 2007	6, 10, 16, 17, 19, 21 January 2009
August 2005	
June 2005	

The UNEP environmental assessment mission used the most recent satellite imagery over the area as well as images covering the area on many different dates. Moreover, at all phases of the project, the information collected was geo-referenced using state-of-the-art technology. The process is described in detail in the following sections.

Stage 1: Damage assessment methodology using detailed satellite imagery over the Gaza Strip

Using commercial satellite images, UNOSAT analysed several images acquired over the Gaza Strip prior to, during and after the hostilities in December 2008 and January 2009.

At the request of various UN agencies, UNOSAT activated its rapid mapping capability at the onset of the fighting and analysed eight satellite image scenes acquired on 6, 10, 16, 17, 19 and 21 January 2009. Satellite imagery that pre-dated the conflict, starting June 2005, was also used (see Table 1). Damage assessments were carried out through standard image interpretation techniques combining automatic and visual inspection methods of imagery acquired at different dates at a reduced spatial resolution of 2 metres. The assessment included damage to buildings, infrastructure, roads, agriculture, and demolition areas.

Affected buildings were classified either as destroyed or severely damaged. Buildings were defined as destroyed if the structure had collapsed totally or, if it was standing, if less than 50 percent of the roof was still intact. Buildings were defined as severely damaged if they had visible structural damage to a portion of at least one wall, or where a section of the roof was damaged but over 50 percent of the roof was still intact. Impact craters on roads and in fields were also assessed. Damage was recorded by type and by estimated occurrence per Governorate (see Table 2).

Table 2.   Summary of impacts detected by governorate

Type of damage	Gaza North	Gaza	Middle Area	Khan Yunis	Rafah	Total per type of damages
Buildings destroyed or severely damaged	585	1,000	95	241	739	2,660
Greenhouses destroyed or severely damaged	58	74	9	25	20	186
Impact craters on road	66	82	13	16	43	220
Impact craters in fields	256	172	59	83	141	711
Total per governorate	965	1,328	176	365	943	**3,777**

Map 3.   Damage analysis map

Legend

Damage density (impacts/km²)

more than 50

between 20 and 50

between 10 and 20

less than 10

Sources: OCHA, UNWRA, GIST, PEQA, UNOSAT.

UNEP PCDMB - 2009

0 1 2 3 4 5 Km

The boundaries and names shown and the designations used on this map do not imply official endorsement by the United Nations.

The limited spatial resolution of the satellite imagery significantly reduces the confidence level for damage identification within dense urban areas. It is highly probable, therefore, that the damage assessment underestimated the actual building and infrastructure damage at the time of satellite image acquisition.

At the time of the damage assessment, limited information from the field was available to verify the remote analysis. Ground survey data and photos were provided by UNEP from its field mission on 30 January 2009. UNOSAT participated in the UN Early Recovery Cluster mission in January-February 2009 to assist coordination and optimize the use of the satellite-derived damage assessment in the recovery process.

The satellite images acquired at different dates during and after the conflict made it possible to detect damage that occurred specifically during the escalation of violence in December 2008-January 2009.

Stage 2: Field maps

Based on the initial damage evaluation, a set of maps was created to assist the field team. It included details of the most severely damaged locations and environmental priority sites (wastewater treatment plants, dumping sites, agro-industrial facilities).

More than 30 detailed location maps at a scale of 1:5,000 were produced for the planned assessment sites, showing all damages and points of interest.

Stage 3: Field data collection

During the mission, experts used handheld Global Positioning System (GPS) devices (Garmin 60 and Garmin Oregon 400) to record the coordinates of sites visited and sampling points. All teams also used GPS-cameras (Nikon CoolPix 6000) with built-in GPS. In total, over 1,500 geo-referenced high-resolution photographs were acquired during the field work. These photos were used to verify the remote images and to share observations between experts after the mission. To facilitate data sharing, all geo-referenced photos were made available to UNEP experts using a web-mapping application developed for the assessment.

2.6 Field work

A. Reconnaissance

Upon arrival in the Gaza Strip, the UNEP team met with representatives of UNDP and the Palestinian EQA and presented the outline of UNEP's plan for field work. Both UNDP and EQA were asked if there were additional areas of environmental concern and/or locations of major environmental impacts that they would like the UNEP team to address. Both parties provided valuable input to the detailed field work plans.

It was important for the UNEP team to obtain as much information as possible about the various types of weapons used so as to understand the possible chemical contamination as well as the presence of UXO. This information was provided by the United Nations Mine Action Service (UNMAS).

The UNEP team then began reconnaissance work in the field, guided by the satellite image maps that had been produced for this purpose by UNOSAT. Guidance was also provided by UNDP staff who accompanied the UNEP team during the field work, and all activity was coordinated with UNDSS. The reconnaissance included the following steps:

- A simple checklist was prepared for carrying out the reconnaissance work; team members noted issues of interest to their field of expertise.

- A GPS reading was taken at each point and photographs (also geo-referenced) were taken.

- The checklists were later used to shortlist the sites for detailed field work and plan for the sampling and monitoring kits to be taken to the individual locations.

The list of sites visited by the UNEP team is provided in Table 3 and the indicative locations are provided in Map 4.

B. Detailed assessment of sites

Based on the reconnaissance work, the UNEP team identified some 30 sites that required sampling and detailed analysis. As mentioned previously, the assessment focused on solid waste, wastewater, and contaminated land. Sampling work was

Table 3.   List of sampling locations

Site #	Location	Site description
1	Northeast Gaza	Juice factory burnt by air attack
2	Northeast Gaza	Cement packing unit damaged during recent events
3	Al Karama Street	Ready-mix concrete damaged by recent events
4	Al Karama Street	Gas station damaged by recent events
5	Northwest Gaza	Beit Lahia sewage lagoon impacted by recent events
6	Northwest Gaza	School damaged by recent action
7	UNDP rubble disposal site	Site for disposal of rubble from 2005 disengagement
8	Tal El Sultan	Waste dumping area reopened during December 2008/wastewater treatment plant
9	South Gaza	Boarder area with Egypt with destroyed housing
10	Southeast Gaza	Ready-mix concrete factory damaged during recent events
11	Southeast Gaza	Unlined sewage site
12	Khan Unis	Lined sewage ponds
13	As Samooni	Impacted agriculture/livestock area
14	Al Salam	Impacted housing area
15	Wadi Gaza	Open drain of sewage to the ground
16	Gaza	Electrical instruments (transformer replaced)
17	Gaza sewage treatment plant	Site of sewage treatment plant
18	Al Sodania	Beach, North Gaza
19	Gaza coastline	Beach near refugee camp
20	Sheikh Ejleen	Sewage outlet into the sea
21	Gaza coastline	Sewage outfall
22	Gaza coastline	Sewage outlet (small)
23	Gaza coastline	Garbage dump near the sea
24	Gaza coastline	Impacted water and sediments from sewage
25	Rafah waste dump	Domestic garbage disposal area, leachate flowing into groundwater
26	Rafah area	Dumping of asbestos and other debris
27	Rafah area	Water wells
28	Gaza coastline	Wastewater outlet into the sea
29	Al Muwasi	Agricultural area
30	Gaza coastline	Sewage disposal close by
31	Gaza coastline	Fishing area
32	Fishing harbour	Fish landing area
33	Gaza City	Al Deira hotel
34	Gaza City	Power plant
35	Gaza	Red Crescent warehouse

adjusted at each site to match the issues that were expected in a given area.

Solid and hazardous waste

The field work followed the rapid assessment methodology used in post-conflict and post-disaster environments. As it was impossible to visit all of the affected sites in the limited amount of time, representative sites were visited and samples were collected to provide recommendations for remediation and restoration.

The field work involved the following steps:

• visits to sites identified by background research or spontaneous investigation of sites passed by during the field trips;

• visual inspection of sites concerning site use, site infrastructure, potential contaminants, obvious damages and obvious contaminations;

• photographic documentation and documentation of issues on site assessment report sheets;

• determination of site coordinates; and

• soil, rubble or waste sampling and sample documentation.

The team also visited various landfills in the area and looked at their state of maintenance and control.

Three different standards were then used as representative international best practice to analyse the quality of soil and waste samples: (i) the Dutch List for the evaluation of soil contamination; (ii) the German LAGA List for the assessment of mineral waste to be used as backfill material; and (iii) the German Sewage Sludge Ordinance (GSSO),[1] which evaluates the acceptability of treated sewage sludge for application on agricultural land.

The LAGA List classifies solid matter (waste) into categories Z0, Z1.1, Z1.2 and Z2, and allows technical use of the various categories under certain circumstances: (Z0) unrestricted use in soil-related conditions; (Z1) restricted use in technical building structures permeable to water, with (Z1.1) being for unfavourable and (Z1.2) for favourable hydrological conditions; and (Z2) restricted use with defined technical safeguard measures.

Waste, including materials from landfill sites, was classified according to the European Waste Catalogue (EWC), which is a list of wastes organized by source and specific production units. Wastes considered to be hazardous are noted in the EWC.

The assessment of waste was carried out with a focus on prevention, including minimizing health hazards for workers and neighbouring communities, as well as preventing contamination arising from waste disposal.

Map 4. Sites visited by the UNEP environmental assessment team

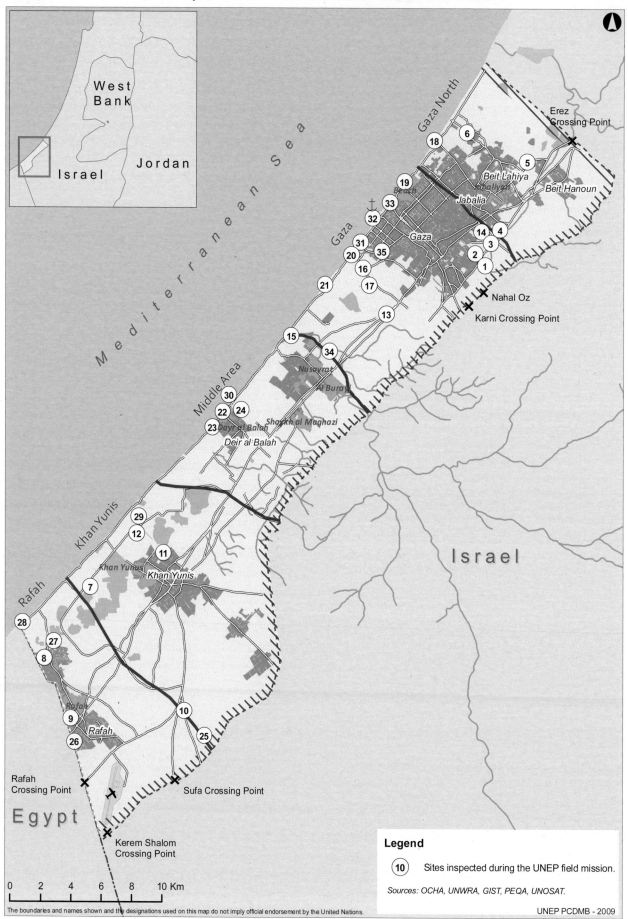

Legend

(10) Sites inspected during the UNEP field mission.

Sources: OCHA, UNWRA, GIST, PEQA, UNOSAT.

The boundaries and names shown and the designations used on this map do not imply official endorsement by the United Nations.

UNEP PCDMB - 2009

Map 5. Agricultural damages by tanks (before)

Cultivated fields

0   150   300
Meters

Acquisition date: 10/01/2009
Copyright: DigitalGlobe

Map 5. Agricultural damages by tanks (after)

Tanks tracks

0   150   300
Meters

Acquisition date: 21/01/2009
Copyright: DigitalGlobe

Map 6.   American International School in Gaza (before)

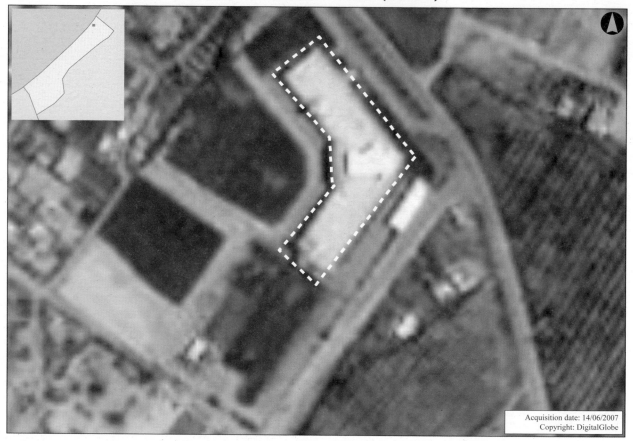

Acquisition date: 14/06/2007
Copyright: DigitalGlobe

Map 6.   American International School in Gaza (after)

Acquisition date: 19/01/2009
Copyright: GeoEye

Map 7.   Rafah border area (before and after)

Egypt

Egypt

0   100   200
Meters

Acquisition date: 10/01/2009
Copyright: DigitalGlobe

Acquisition date: 21/01/2009
Copyright: DigitalGlobe

Asbestos assessment

At each location that was visited, the UNEP team made a brief inspection of the site on foot. Where materials that were suspected of containing asbestos were observed, location details were recorded both on paper and using a digital camera with a GPS. A representative sample was taken using appropriate hand tools and techniques. The potential for asbestos fibre release during sampling was minimized by the use of a dust-suppressing water spray where required. Each sample was then sealed in labelled polythene bags and sent to a laboratory in Switzerland for analysis for asbestos type.

Frequently observed and/or visibly similar materials were not sampled at every site. If a sampled material was found to contain asbestos, other materials of the same general type, appearance and usage were assumed to contain asbestos. Where building materials were visibly consistent with materials that did not contain asbestos, such as plasterboard or fibreglass, a visual observation and note was made, and no samples were taken for analysis.

As part of health and safety precautions for the UNEP assessment, an air sampling investigation was also carried out for asbestos. Team members were fitted with pumps that drew air from the breathing zone of the individual. To comply with the WHO standard method, an open-faced filter holder with an electrically conducting cylindrical cowl and exposed

Asbestos in rubble

area of filter at least 20 mm in diameter was used for sampling. The filter holder was fixed to the clothing as close to the mouth and nose as was practicable, and was always within 200 mm of the breathing zone.

A measured volume of air was then drawn through a cellulose ester membrane filter fixed within a filter head by means of a sampling pump. After the air samples had been taken, all the filters were returned to the United Kingdom (UK) for laboratory analysis. Each filter was mounted on a microscope slide and rendered transparent. Respirable fibres on a measured area of the filter were counted using x500 magnification phase contrast microscopy (PCM). Respirable fibres to be counted were defined as any particle with a length of >5 μm, a width of <3 μm and having an aspect ratio (length:width ratio) of >3:1, as prescribed by the Health and Safety document "HSG248" (*Asbestos: The analysts' guide for sampling analysis and clearance procedures*).

The fibre count from PCM analysis may not be able to resolve fibres with widths <0.2 μm and, therefore, represents only a proportion of the total number of fibres present. This means that the airborne fibre concentration level is only an index of the numerical concentration of fibres and not an absolute measure of the total number of fibres present. As this method alone is unable to discriminate between asbestos and non-asbestos fibres, all fibres meeting the size definition above were counted.

UNEP expert in Rafah with asbestos samples

Environmental Assessment of the Gaza Strip

Water-related issues

The main water-related issues covered during the field work were:

- **Damage to the water supply and sewage system** caused by the hostilities, and related damage to water supply sources (wells). The team assessed various systems established for the handling of sewage and storm water infiltration, which were originally designed as separate systems but had in most cases become partly or fully connected through modifications and breakages.

- **Water quality in the Gaza Strip.** The sole water supply source of the Gaza Strip is the coastal aquifer, but there is variation in water quality in different locations. Water is abstracted from the aquifer for drinking, and for commercial and agricultural purposes. The UNEP team collected water from wells used for irrigation, as well as from the municipal supply. Samples from commercial sources of drinking water (tankered and bottled water) were also gathered.

- **Sewage disposal**, including the discharge of partially or entirely untreated sewage into the Mediterranean Sea. In some locations, raw sewage flows into the sea as an open drain, the most prominent example being Wadi Gaza. Seawater samples were collected where

sewage was being discharged into the sea. Due to security constraints, it was considered unsafe to undertake sampling in deeper seawaters.

To test water quality in the Gaza Strip during the field mission, the UNEP team used a Hach water quality testing meter to obtain screening-level values for salinity and pH. Samples collected were tested with multiple electrodes to obtain the required values. An interface meter (Heron dipper-T water level meter) was employed to determine the depth of the water column in a well, which made it possible to differentiate between floating hydrocarbons and the water level below.

The results of groundwater samples were compared against WHO guidelines for drinking water quality, given that all the water was drawn from the same aquifer and, in the absence of official controls or regulations, any source of water available in the Gaza Strip could potentially be consumed by the population, including water from private wells. Seawater samples were compared against WHO Guidelines for Safe Recreational Waters (WHO 2003). Water samples from sewage treatment plants were compared against Palestinian guidelines for effluent quality from sewage treatment plants.

Land contamination and degradation

The original assessment plan was to study land contamination. However, it became evident during the reconnaissance visit that not only were there

Demolished gasoline station in Northern Gaza Strip

potentially contaminated sites, but that several areas were also seriously degraded.

Contamination: The escalation of violence caused pockets of contamination, such as hydrocarbon contamination at industrial sites, sewage contamination around broken storage tanks, continuing sewage contamination around sewage treatment plants, storm water infiltration areas, and contaminated sewage drains and coastline. Furthermore, because both the weapons used and the materials present within the buildings had chemical constituents, it had to be assumed that every damaged site, including impacted agricultural areas, was also potentially contaminated.

The assessment of land contamination was carried out based on the model of contaminant source–pathway–receptor. This model posits that a contamination hazard exists only when all three factors are present: a contaminant at a source (e.g. groundwater contamination) can only reach the receptor (e.g. human being) if there is a pathway (e.g. drinking water well). If there is no pathway, or no receptor, there is no immediate hazard. On the other hand, the risk of contamination cannot be ruled out, so it is recommended to preventively protect soil and groundwater from contamination by industrial or commercial activities.

Degradation: Extensive areas of orchards and farmland were seriously physically degraded by the movement of ground forces. The UNEP team collected samples of soil from locations of visible suspected contamination. Observations and photographs of land degradation were also taken.

C. Economic and institutional assessment

The UNEP mandate included an economic calculation of the cost of restoration. The field team, therefore, carried out interviews with site owners to understand the nature of their ownership, type of losses involved and the compensation they had received, if any. The team also conducted interviews with UN experts and Palestinian Authority officials to understand the institutional capacity in the Gaza Strip for environmental assessment and restoration. Information required for the costing of the various sectors (land, water, solid wastes) was also collected.

2.7 Laboratory analysis

All samples were collected in triplicate. One set was given to the EQA of the Palestinian Authority and another was shared with the Israeli Ministry of Environment. UNEP shipped the third set of samples to Switzerland for analysis at Bachema AG Analytical Laboratory. Asbestos samples were analysed at the specialized Carbotech Laboratory in Switzerland. Fish samples were analysed at GBA Fruit Analytic GMBH, in Sweden.

2.8 Limitations and constraints

Over 3,000 sites in the Gaza Strip were impacted by the escalation of hostilities in December 2008 and January 2009. It was not this assessment's objective to visit all impacted sites, nor was this feasible in the time available. As mentioned above, a set of representative sites was selected based on remote sensing and background research to understand the key impacts.

UNEP received access to most affected sites within the Gaza Strip, but there were some exceptions. For example, it was evident from satellite image analysis that the movement of ground forces within the first 500 metres of the Green Line inside the Gaza Strip had caused land degradation. This area remained inaccessible to the UNEP team.

In addition, the UNEP team did not collect offshore samples due to restrictions imposed by the Israeli navy for security reasons. While it was theoretically possible to obtain special permission to conduct field work in the sea, there were no marked UN vessels available and it was considered unsafe to venture out in unmarked boats.

Finally, while the Palestinian Authority had in the past carried out regular sampling to test groundwater quality at hundreds of wells, the current internal political situation in the Gaza Strip prevented their staff from accompanying the UNEP team to act as guides and from providing the coordinates of wells. The UNEP team was, therefore, obliged to seek and sample water wells in an ad hoc fashion. The institutional disarray in the Gaza Strip also limited the team's access to pre-existing data.

3   Results and discussions

3.1   Introduction

It is clear from this assessment that the environment in the Gaza Strip following the escalation of violence in December 2008 and January 2009 is severely degraded. In some environmental sectors, the hostilities caused direct damage that was clearly distinguishable by satellite image analysis, reports from other UN agencies, visual inspection of the age of the damage, and chemical analysis. In others, recent events played a contributory role, exacerbating environmental degradation that existed prior to the violence. This chapter seeks to differentiate between damages that can be directly attributed to the recent hostilities and environmental degradation that was aggravated by them. It should be noted, however, that it was not always scientifically possible to make this differentiation. An evaluation of the institutions, systems and equipment currently in place for environmental management in the Gaza Strip is also provided, with a view to identifying needs and priorities for reconstruction.

3.2   Damages directly attributable to the recent escalation of violence

Construction and demolition waste

The most obvious impact of the recent escalation of hostilities is the large quantity of demolition debris that was generated in the Gaza Strip. As

Complete results and detailed laboratory reports of the sample analyses conducted can be accessed at:

http:/postconflict.unep.ch/gaza_samples

noted above, satellite imagery shows that 2,692 buildings were impacted; some of these buildings were completely destroyed, while others were partially damaged and rendered unsafe. UNDP estimates that the total quantity of demolition debris produced during this period was close to 600,000 tonnes.

Available data from UN organizations does not distinguish between residential buildings and industrial or commercial buildings, so it is difficult to evaluate how many of these locations may contain hazardous materials. Nevertheless, there is a high probability that most building rubble is contaminated to some degree, including from residential buildings, where household hazardous materials (disinfectants, medicines, solvents, etc.) are present.

In addition, a number of buildings were hit by ammunition that caused fires and partial or total destruction of the structure. Building fires contaminate the building and/or the resulting rubble with polynuclear aromatic hydrocarbons (PAHs) and, if chlorinated compounds are present, with dioxins and furans, all of which are extremely hazardous.

Burnt out interior of the Red Crescent building in Gaza City

Table 4. Ash sample, Red Crescent building, Gaza City

Parameter	RC-SOIL-01 (mg/kg)	LAGA Z values (mg/kg)
Al	9,280	N/A
Mg	11,900	N/A
P	420	N/A
Zn	15,300	>Z2 (>1,500 mg/kg)
Sb	356	N/A
Pb	13.1	Z0 (<40 mg/kg)
Cu	43.0	Z1 (<120 mg/kg)
Ni	24.5	Z1 (<150 mg/kg)
Hg	0.13	Z1 (<1.5 mg/kg)
ΣPAH	19.6	Z2 (<30 mg/kg)
Naphthalene	6.5	N/A
Phenantrene	6.1	N/A
Phenols	0.3	N/A
	RC-SOIL-01 (ng/kg)	SPCSO action value GSSO limit value (ng/kg)
2,3,7,8-TCDD[a]	0.2	N/A
TE-NATO[b]	34.7	100

EWC: 17 07 02[c]: Mixed construction and demolition waste or separated fractions containing dangerous substances

[a] 2,3,7,8-TCDD ("Seveso dioxin")
[b] NATO toxicity equivalent, in multiples of 2,3,7,8-TCDD toxicity
[c] hazardous waste according to EWC
N/A = not applicable

Table 5. Rubble dust sample, bombed building, Al Shati Camp, Gaza City

Parameter	19-SOIL-01 [mg/kg]	LAGA Z Values [mg/kg]
pH (water)	8.5	Z0 (>6.5/<9.5)
Al	7,350	N/A
Mg	3,370	N/A
P	380	N/A
Cr	13.4	Z0 (<30)
Zn	55.6	Z0 (<60)
Cu	9.7	Z0 (<20)
Ni	10.3	Z0 (<15)
ΣPAH	0.05	Z0 (<3)
Pyrene	0.05	N/A
Trinitrobenzene-1,3,5	0.001	N/A
Octogen (HMX)	0.004	N/A
	RC-SOIL-01 [ng/kg]	SPCSO Action Value GSSO Limit Value [ng/kg]
2,3,7,8-TCDD*	<1.0	N/A
TE-NATO**	<0.2	100

EWC: 17 07 02*: Mixed construction and demolition waste or separated fractions containing dangerous substances

* 2,3,7,8-TCDD ("Seveso dioxin")
** NATO toxicity equivalent, in multiples of 2,3,7,8-TCDD toxicity
*** hazardous waste according to EWC, due to the presence of asbestos (discussed in other chapter)
N/A: not applicable

For example, the UNEP assessment team investigated a Red Crescent building in Gaza City that had been used as a storage facility for medical equipment and pharmaceuticals and, according to UNDP anecdotal evidence, had burned for more than 48 hours. Due to the heat of the fire, reinforced concrete supports had split and the building appeared structurally unsafe. The walls and supports were scorched, and there was an unmistakable smell of PAHs inside the building. The team collected a mixed sample from ash inside the building; the analysis results are shown in Table 4.

Although aluminium, magnesium and phosphorous concentrations appear high, they are in the range that would be expected in wood ash arising from burning of wooden shelves, interior wooden sheeting and construction materials. Phosphorous bombs, which were reportedly used during the recent hostilities, often cause fires. In the present instance, however, a close relationship between the observed levels of phosphorous and the possible use of such bombs cannot be concluded. The most serious heavy metal contamination in the ash results from zinc (Zn: 15,300 mg/kg) and metalloids from antimony (Sb: 356 mg/kg). These are critical levels of concentration in the

environment if they are deposited openly on waste dump sites. Though it is plausible that they originate from burnt medicines, the source of these elements cannot be determined with certainty.

PAH concentrations in the ash sample are not alarmingly high, yet the volatile nature of the naphthalene it contains may render the building useless for future use as a food storage area, as planned by the Red Crescent. Due to the contamination by soot and smoke, the storage of foodstuffs cannot be recommended without complete remediation and clean-up. It is recommended to use the building as a parking garage or repair workshop instead.

Another example of the danger posed by the rubble generated by the recent hostilities is a destroyed house in the Al Shati Camp, situated on the coast 1.5 km north of Gaza City harbour. According to local people, children complained about headaches and skin irritations after playing in the rubble.

The rubble dust was sampled and tested for various parameters related to rubble, waste, and explosives. The results of the analysis are shown in Table 5.

Based on these results, the rubble could be classified as Z0, i.e. it is suitable for technical construction purposes without restriction. However, in all such situations, close attention should be paid during the removal process to the possible presence of asbestos and other hazardous materials. If these are encountered, they should be sorted out onsite, stored separately and transported to a suitable hazardous waste facility.

Finally so-called "hanging rubble," caused by the aerial bombing of buildings of two or more storeys, presents a considerable problem. Hanging rubble is unstable, and may fall at any time. Buildings damaged in this manner are unsafe to enter because of the risk of collapse.

Under normal circumstances, these buildings could be demolished with high-reach nibbler cranes, which can work at heights of more than 60 metres. However, these machines are not available in the Gaza Strip.

Demolition by blasting cannot be carried out for safety reasons, as the buildings are not sound enough for preparation work such as the weakening of pillars. A controlled explosion is not feasible either, as structural weaknesses and uneven distribution of mass make it impossible to produce a controlled collapse, and secondary damage might occur to neighbouring houses in Gaza City's densely populated communities. For obvious safety reasons, it is also impossible to demolish the buildings by hand.

However, the problem urgently requires a solution which, considering the special circumstances in the Gaza Strip, should ideally not only be low tech and low cost, but also in line with international standards of work health and safety. It is therefore recommended to engage a professional health and safety expert to assist the teams undertaking the demolition.

Hanging rubble in partially demolished buildings, like this one in Gaza City, poses a major challenge

Hazardous waste

In a conflict situation, hazardous waste can be generated either from the materials stored in a structure that is damaged or by the weapons used to cause the damage. Many different activities use hazardous substances as base materials, or generate hazardous waste. If explosives are used to destroy a building and contaminate the demolition debris, the debris must be treated as hazardous waste. In addition, explosives can cause fires, which can also generate hazardous waste.

Evidence of hazardous materials, albeit in small quantities, was observed at a number of locations during UNEP site visits. At the El Swaity juice and food production factory in the Beit Lahia area in northern Gaza Strip, the cooling warehouse had been hit by a bomb and had burst into flames. The fire was further fuelled by flammable Styrofoam insulation. The contents of the warehouse burned away completely, leaving soot, ash, tar and burnt organic substances in the debris.

Thus, the debris can be considered contaminated with PAHs and probably with polychlorinated biphenyls (PCBs), dioxins and furans as well. Demolition of the building requires personal protective equipment, which is not readily available in the Gaza Strip.

There were many other sites of small-scale industries in the Gaza Strip, which the UNEP team could not all visit or investigate. However, during the clean-up operation, each of these sites will need to be treated as potentially containing hazardous materials.

In addition, fuel stations and tanks were routinely targeted during the military operations. Accordingly, UNEP visited three sites to assess potential soil contamination from fuel:

- a poultry farm that operated its groundwater pump with a diesel aggregate that was fuelled by a 100 litre tank that had been completely destroyed;

- a gasoline station that was completely destroyed above ground, with the 8 x 30 m³ tanks still intact; some soil contamination occurred when the owner of the gasoline station tried to sell gasoline in spite of his destroyed infrastructure and spilled 10-20 litres of diesel on the concrete floor; and

- a cement factory in Rafah that had stored approximately 1,000 litres of diesel for its trucks in a tank that was destroyed.

The results of analyses of samples taken from these three locations are shown in Table 6.

Table 6.   Soil analysis of Az Zaitoun poultry farm (03-SOIL-01), Beit Hanoun gasoline station (04-SOIL-01) and Rafah ready-mix cement plant (10-SOIL-01)

Parameter	03-SOIL-01 (mg/kg)	04-SOIL-01 (mg/kg)	10-SOIL-01 (mg/kg)	Dutch List (mg/kg)
	Poultry farm	Gasoline station	Cement factory	Intervention values
Total petroleum hydrocarbons (TPHs)	7,560	12,600	N/D	5,000
Hydrocarbons >C40	>20	<20	N/D	N/A
Aliphatic hydrocarbons (C5-C10)	<500	1,770	5,010	(5,000)
Benzene	<5	6	<5	1
Toluene	<5	44	<5	130
Ethylbenzene	<5	<5	<5	50
Xylene (m,p)	<5	28	<5	25
Xylene (o)	<5	18	10	
Sum BTEX	<10	96	<10	N/A
Sum PAH (EPA)	N/A	N/A	N/A	40
Size of tank(s)	1x100 litres	8x30 m³	1x1,000 litres	N/A
Tanks damaged/spill	yes/100%	none/<1%, secondary	yes/100%	N/A

N/A = not applicable
N/D = no data

Environmental Assessment of the Gaza Strip

Bulldozed cement plant near Rafah

In all three cases, soil contamination by TPHs/aliphatic hydrocarbons – and benzene in the gasoline station – exceed the intervention values of the Dutch List. In the case of the poultry farm, it is highly recommended that the soil be excavated (<10 m³) and relocated, as the spill occurred immediately beside a groundwater well. There is a distinct risk that the well will be contaminated when rainfall intensifies in December and January and that the contaminants will reach the groundwater. The gasoline station spill is less significant, as only a few litres of diesel were spilled, and they were spilled on a concrete surface and absorbed by loose sand and silt. The spill is no more serious than spills that occur during normal gasoline station operations. The soil surface is sealed, and there is little risk of fuel being carried to the groundwater.

The cement factory in Rafah was completely destroyed, including trucks and storage silos. The area affected by the spill comprises some 10-20 m². The spill site presents no immediate hazard, as the volatile substances have apparently already evaporated. The spillage area should be excavated and can be cleaned up as described above with regard to the poultry farm.

Overall, the total quantity of hazardous waste generated by this recent escalation of hostilities does not appear to be significant. In the absence of a dedicated facility to handle hazardous waste, however, there is a concern that such waste will be disposed of with non-hazardous waste, thereby contaminating landfills. There is therefore a long-term need to create a system for hazardous waste management in the Gaza Strip.

Dead animals

According to the Palestinian National Early Recovery and Reconstruction Plan for Gaza 2009-2010,[2] over 35,750 cattle, sheep and goats and more than one million birds and chickens were killed during the recent events. These animals could not be consumed for religious and hygiene reasons. The owner of a damaged stable that the UNEP assessment team visited in May 2009 in a commercial/agricultural area east of Jabaliyah stated that he had lost more than 200 goats and sheep during the attack, which severely damaged his stable. He stated that the municipality of Gaza had ordered him to bury the animals and cover them with lime. Nevertheless, close to the site, many animal cadavers could still be seen lying unattended as late as May 2009. Although the total mass of cadavers can only be estimated, it appears to range between 1,000 and 1,500 tonnes.

Dead animals at the roadside in Beit Hanoun

Farmers rehabilitating an olive plantation bulldozed during operation Cast Lead, east of Gaza City

Damage to farmland and orchards

The recent escalation of hostilities led to the large-scale destruction of farmland, including orchards, greenhouses and open fields. The movement of large military vehicles over agricultural land affected the texture of the soil. Before 27 December 2008, the total cultivated area in the Gaza Strip was recorded as 170,000,000 m^2 or 170,000 dunum (158,000,000 m^2 open field and 12,000,000 m^2 greenhouses).[3] According to an agricultural survey conducted by UNDP/PAPP, 17 percent of the total cultivated area of the Gaza Strip was completely destroyed in the conflict, including 17.5 percent of the orchards and 9.2 percent of open fields.[4]

The Gaza Strip is ecologically very vulnerable, as almost all agricultural land is situated within a few kilometres of desert-like sand dunes. Agriculture in the Gaza Strip is only sustained by the very delicate handling of the land by the farming community, which has generations of accumulated knowledge. The recent destruction of the vegetation cover has degraded the land in several ways. First, the mechanical ripping and removal of trees, shrubs and crops has moved, mixed and thinned the topsoil cover over large

areas. This degradation of the top productive layer will impact future cultivation of the land. Second, the passage of heavy tracked vehicles has compacted the soil into a dense crust, which will need to be tilled with heavy ploughing machinery to make it suitable for agriculture again. Such machinery is not currently available in the Gaza Strip. Third, the destruction of the vegetation cover will make the land vulnerable to desertification. Destruction of tree cover will also accelerate soil erosion during rainfall. Finally, it may not be possible for the farmers to grow the same crops or reforest the damaged areas, as the salinity of the water used for irrigation has increased significantly in some parts of the Gaza Strip in recent years. Young fruit and olive saplings are less tolerant of brackish water and while mature plants would have survived due to slow adaptation to rising salinity, new crops may not be able to develop. The cumulative impact of these various forms of degradation is a high cost of restoration and a long-term reduction in agricultural productivity.

According to the UNOSAT assessment, a number of impact craters can be found in open areas, some of which is farmland. These sites need to be treated as potentially contaminated and should be assessed before the area is cleared for reuse.

Land degradation around Az Zaitoun wastewater treatment plant

The Az Zaitoun wastewater treatment plant, generally known as the Gaza wastewater treatment plant, was constructed in stages:

- 1977: two pond treatment system (anaerobic ponds);

- 1986: two additional ponds (aerated pond and polishing pond – 12,000 m³/day);

- 1994: rehabilitation by UNRWA (without increasing capacity);

- 1998: upgrade and expansion to 32,000 m³/day (by the United States Agency for International Development); and

- 2008: 45,000-55,000 m³/day.

There are further plans to upgrade the plant to a hydraulic capacity of 90,000 m³/day. According to the Gaza Coastal Municipalities Water Utility (CMWU),[5] the plant comprises:

- anaerobic ponds no. 1 and no. 2: 91 m x 81 m, water depth 4.3 m, volume 20,000 m³ each;

- 1 effluent polishing pond: 99 m x 63 m, water depth 4.5 m, volume 20,600 m³;

- anaerobic pond no. 3: 164 m x 76 m, water depth 5.2 m, volume 32,000 m³;

- 2 bio-towers (trickling towers): 26 m diameter, 7.3 m filter media height, volume 3,862 m³ each;

- 1 aeration pond: 184 m x 76 m, water depth 4.6 m, volume 38,000 m³;

- 1 sludge holding pond: 85 m x 51 m, water depth 4.5 m, volume 2,800 m³, holding time nine days;

- settling pond: 66 m x 13.5 m, water depth 5.8 m, volume 2,200 m³; and

- 8 sludge drying beds: 50 m x 24 m, water depth 1 m, daily sludge load 300 m³, drying time ten days.

Figure 1 shows the setting and layout of the plant.

Figure 1.　　Layout of the Az Zaitoun wastewater treatment plant[5]

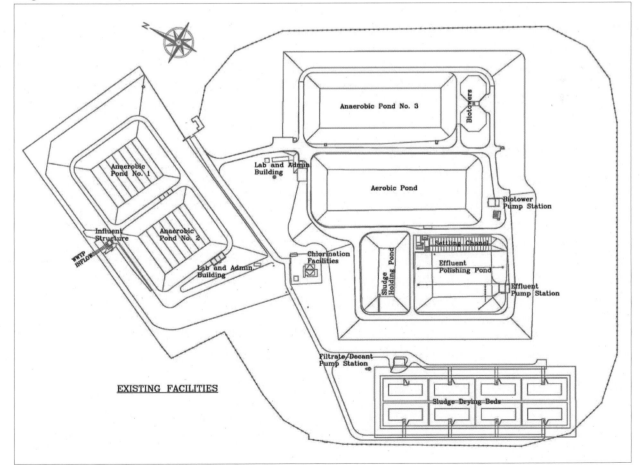

During the recent conflict, anaerobic pond no. 3 was damaged, its embankment destroyed, and more than 100,000 m³ of wastewater and sludge spilled into adjacent agricultural areas.[6] UNDP estimated that 55,000 square metres of agricultural land were impacted by this spill.

At the time of the visit, the sludge had dried and was spread over a large area. Map 9 shows the extent of the spread of sewage and where sludge had settled, several inches deep. To investigate the impact on soil quality, samples were taken at a location where sewage sludge was still visible, a field approximately 100 metres northeast of anaerobic basin no. 1. The samples comprised dried wastewater sludge on top of the soil with a thickness of 2-5 cm (17-SOIL-01), top soil at a depth of 2-5 cm (17-SOIL-02) and soil beneath at a depth of 5-10 cm (17-SOIL-01) (see Table 7).

Untreated (and even partly treated) sewage sludge contains large quantities of pathogens as well as elevated levels of heavy metals. In most countries, the disposal of sewage sludge is regulated based on its quality, the quantity to be applied and the type of land where it might be applied. The uncontrolled spreading of untreated sewage and settling of sewage sludge

Plants growing on dried sewage sludge near Az Zaitoun plant

Table 7. Analysis of Az Zaitoun samples

Parameter	17-SOIL-01 (mg/kg)	LAGA List (mg/kg)
	Sewage sludge, surface	Z value
pH of soil	N/A	N/A
$C_{org.}$	N/D	N/A
Mg	6,750	N/A
Al	14,900	N/A
P	4,800	N/A
Pb	130	Z1 (<210)
Cd	0.8	Z1 (<3)
Cr	66	Z1 (<180)
Co	<10.0	N/A
Cu	210	Z2 (<400)
Ni	32.2	Z1 (<150)
Hg	2.23	Z 2 (<5)
Zn	1,220	Z2 (<1,500)

[a] According to EWC: 19 08 Wastes from wastewater treatment plants not otherwise specified, 19 08 05 sludge from treatment of urban wastewater.
N/A = not applicable
N/D = no data

on agricultural land is therefore unacceptable and needs to be corrected if reference levels (e.g. according to the GSSO) are superseded. In the current situation, the sewage sludge also exceeds the German LAGA List for waste classification. The site itself should be reinvestigated prior to new crops being grown in the area.

Impacts to water supply and sewage networks

In addition to the serious damage created by the breakage of the embankment at Az Zaitoun, a number of other parts of the water supply and sewage system were affected during the hostilities. This includes impacts to water wells, the water distribution network, sewage collection network and water tanks. Many facilities had been repaired by the time the UNEP team was on the ground but a good description of the damage is provided in a report by the CMWU in 2009 (*Damage assessment report: Water and wastewater infrastructure and facilities, 27 December 2008 – 19 January 2009, Gaza*). At the time of the visit, UNEP observed damaged water supply wells.

Map 8.   Az Zaitoun sewage treatment plant breach of embankment

Acquisition date: 14/06/2007
Copyright: DigitalGlobe

Acquisition date: 19/01/2009
Copyright: DigitalGlobe

25-30 m

UNEP field mission photo
Date: 31/01/2009
UNEP PCDMB - 2009

Map 9. Extent of sewage flood from Az Zaitoun sewage treatment plant

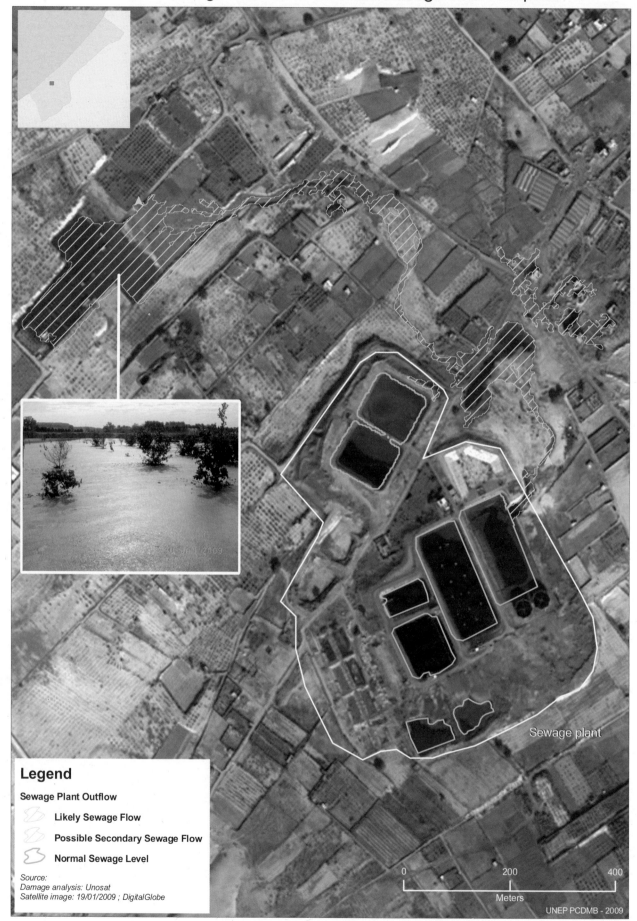

Legend

Sewage Plant Outflow

Likely Sewage Flow

Possible Secondary Sewage Flow

Normal Sewage Level

Source:
Damage analysis: Unosat
Satellite image: 19/01/2009 ; DigitalGlobe

Sewage plant

0   200   400
Meters

UNEP PCDMB - 2009

Environmental Assessment of the Gaza Strip

Asbestos

During UNEP's mission to the Gaza Strip in January 2009, asbestos was observed in several buildings that had been destroyed during the recent events. Limited sampling undertaken at that time also confirmed the presence of asbestos in some areas. The assessment mission in May 2009 therefore included an international asbestos expert. During the mission, asbestos was observed to be present in a number of locations. The other key observations were the following:

- Asbestos was routinely observed in comparatively older buildings and often in buildings with temporary extensions and sheds.

- Industrial buildings used for livestock facilities routinely had asbestos roofing and side walls.

- Generally, no suspected asbestos-containing materials were observed during inspections of buildings and structures of more recent construction, although this does not guarantee that they will not be found during the demolition of these buildings.

- A significant amount of asbestos cement debris was noted in areas where it was not possible to identify the original source of the material. This debris was possibly from buildings that had been demolished in the past, and the asbestos cement had not been removed with the other debris. In some cases, the asbestos cement debris appeared to have been taken to the area and then dumped.

- All the landfills visited by the team showed evidence that asbestos had been dumped in them, indicating that there is neither awareness nor control over asbestos disposal in the Gaza Strip, though it is impossible to attribute this to the recent conflict.

Samples were taken from a variety of locations; the results are shown in Table 8. All the samples taken

Table 8.   Asbestos sampling location and type

Sampling location	Asbestos present	Type of asbestos
11	Yes	Chrysotile Crocidolite
13	Yes	Chrysotile
17	Yes	Chrysotile Crocidolite
21	Yes	Chrysotile Crocidolite
25	Yes	Chrysotile
26	Yes	Chrysotile
32	Yes	Chrysotile Crocidolite

from the various sites tested positive for asbestos. More worryingly, some locations tested positive for crocidolite (blue asbestos), which is generally considered to be 500 times more carcinogenic than chrysotile (white asbestos).

Materials that appeared to be asbestos cement sheets were noted in several locations – generally, industrial and agricultural buildings. As some removal of demolition debris was already taking place, the UNEP team conducted two asbestos awareness training sessions for those involved in the removal during its mission to the Gaza Strip.

The results of the air testing were compared against the UK Control of Asbestos Regulations 2006 (L143) "control limits," which establish internationally accepted safety limits for asbestos in air. The control limit is a respirable concentration of asbestos in the air averaged over any continuous period to which employees must not be exposed unless they are wearing suitable respiratory protective equipment. The control limit is specified as 0.1 fibres/cubic centimetre of air averaged over any continuous period of four hours for any form of asbestos, either alone or in mixtures, including mixtures of chrysotile with any other form of asbestos. The results obtained from the samples taken during the various site activities described above indicate that the control limits for asbestos were not exceeded (see Table 9).

Table 9.   Air sampling investigation findings

Sample number	Sample type	Location	Sample volume (litres)	Limits of detection (fibres/cm³)	Fibre concentration (fibres/cm³)
1	Personal	On Muralee Thummarukudy during site assessment	558	0.0086	<0.0086
2	Personal	On David Smith during site assessment	898	0.0053	<0.0053
3	Personal	On Joanne Stutz during site assessment	279	0.0200	<0.0200

UNEP expert with a sampling pump for occupational asbestos exposure

The results indicate that levels for all respirable fibres (the examination being non-discriminatory regarding fibre type) were very low in comparison to the UK control limit and may be indicative of a local ambient environmental level. However, it is recommended that such air quality surveys be carried out during demolition work, when the chances of breakage of asbestos and release of fibres are high. This survey was carried out to monitor occupational exposure to asbestos and is not relevant to the exposure of the general public to asbestos.

3.3 Environmental issues pre-dating the recent escalation of hostilities that were aggravated by it

As discussed previously, the Gaza Strip's environment was faced with a number of challenges prior to the recent escalation of hostilities. The following section describes environmental issues that were exacerbated by the recent events, but cannot be solely imputed to them. While it was possible to demonstrate the linkages between the hostilities and the degradation in these environmental sectors, it was not possible to measure the exact

proportion of the damage that is attributable to the recent violence. However, the improvement of the state of the environment in the Gaza Strip, and indeed in the region, can only be achieved if the situation in these key sectors is addressed.

Sewage-related contamination

Sewage management – including the collection, treatment and disposal of sewage – has been a major environmental challenge in the Gaza Strip for several decades. Recent reports indicate that 60 percent of the population now lives in areas with sewage networks, while the remainder uses septic tanks and cesspits (Ashour et al., 2009). Due to low per capita water consumption, the sewage in the Gaza Strip is highly concentrated, with typical influent levels of biological oxygen demand (BOD) of up to 600 mg/litre as compared to 250 mg/litre, which is standard for urban sewage. Given that the three existing wastewater treatment plants function only intermittently, little sewage is treated and most is returned to lagoons, wadis and the sea: along the Gaza Strip, 16 outfalls discharge directly into the sea, including Wadi Gaza, which discharges up to 70,000-80,000 cubic metres per day (see Table 10).

Sewage systems were impacted in several ways during the hostilities. First, as the electricity supply collapsed, transfer pumps ceased to function, resulting in sewage being diverted to the nearest available lagoons, including infiltration lagoons. Second, the limited treatment that had been taking place in sewage treatment plants also ceased due to electricity shortages. The effluent leaving sewage treatment plants to be disposed of in the sea or by infiltration in the groundwater was therefore entirely untreated.

Regular monitoring of the sewage treatment plants is no longer conducted, so there is no efficiency data available for most wastewater treatment plants. Recent data (CMWU 2009) on Gaza wastewater treatment plant shows an inflow BOD of 415 mg/litre and effluent BOD of 172 mg/litre, with 58 percent efficiency. Government records also show that treatment efficiency declined from 89 percent in 2007 to 73 percent in 2008.

UNEP collected sewage data at nine locations ranging from a treatment basin to final disposal points. Results of ammonia, chemical oxygen demand (COD) and coliforms are presented in Table 11, along with permissible levels for groundwater infiltration and sea outflow.

As Table 11 shows, none of the sewage samples are fit for infiltration or marine disposal, which are the two alternative methods of sewage disposal currently used in the Gaza Strip. The related contamination of both the groundwater and seawater is discussed further on.

Table 10.   Management of sewage in the Gaza Strip

Parameter	Name of governorate				
	Rafah	Khan Yunis	Middle governorate	Gaza	North Gaza
Population	184,000	250,000	190,000	470,000	445,000
Total sewage collected	8,500	5,000	None	60,000	17,000
Sewage treatment plant	Yes	Partly to treatment, partly to storm water lagoon	None	Yes	Yes
Method	Treatment lagoons	Aerobic and anaerobic lagoons	No treatment	Aerobic and anaerobic lagoons and bio-towers	Aerobic, anaerobic lagoons and polishing ponds
Capacity	4,000	N/D	N/D	50,000	5,000
Type of disposal	Pipeline to sea	Infiltration to ground	Wadi Gaza	Disposed to sea	35-hectare holding lake

N/D = no data

Table 11.   Concentration of key parameters in sewage samples

	Chemical concentration		
WHO guideline for infiltration	Ammonia (mg/l)	COD (mg/l)	E. Coli (cfu/100ml)
	5	150	1,000
WHO guideline for marine disposal	10	200	50,000
Sample reference			
5 water 01	92.4	416	>10,000
8 water 01	185	1,770	12,600
8 water 02	135	3,440	>10,000
11 water 01	74.7	451	25,200
15 water 01	76.4	1,470	>10,000
17 water 01	N/D	1	<10
21 water 01	65.2	761	>10,000
25 water 01	N/D	78	150
28 water 01	135	280	14,000

N/D = no data

Beit Lahia wastewater treatment plant (Site no. 5)

Beit Lahia wastewater treatment plant is located some 1.5 km east of Beit Lahia town centre, with the closest buildings only 50 metres away from the plant. It was constructed in stages:

- 1989: start of construction by Israeli military order (capacity: 50,000 inhabitants);

- 1991: expansion with UNDP assistance to 5,000 m³/day;

- 2003: capacity increased to 10,000 m³/day; and

- 2009: 17,000 m³/day (EWASH 2009).

In 2003, 90 percent of the population of Jabaliyah, 60 percent of Beit Hanoun and 40 percent of Beit Lahia were connected to the plant, but even at that time the wastewater received by the plant greatly exceeded its capacity. As there is no outlet into the sea, wastewater flows into the surrounding dune areas, creating a sewage lake of approximately 450,000 m² (45 hectares or 450 dunums). The sewage lake is expected to expand further, as water infiltration and transmission underground decrease due to the declining permeability of the layer of sewage sediment. This anticipated expansion poses an immediate threat to the neighbouring population downstream. In March 2007, the sewage lake broke its embankment and flooded part of the Bedouin village of Um Al Nasser. Five people drowned, and 1,800 people (280 families) had to be evacuated from the flooded village. As the management of the sewage lake depends on working pumps, fuel shortages also threaten the population, as demonstrated during the recent crisis. In addition, the sewage lake is an ideal breeding ground for mosquitoes and water-borne diseases.

Three soil samples were collected at this site in order to evaluate contamination from the storage of sewage on land (05-SOIL-01 and 05-SOIL-02). An additional sample was taken from an effluent lake that formed below the uppermost basin to the south of Beit Lahia wastewater treatment plant.

The soil was analysed for various heavy metals, as well as for groups of organic contaminants. None of the parameters analysed was found in concentrations that gave reason for concern, thus a comparison with the Dutch List and the LAGA List was not carried out at this site.

In addition to chemical analysis, grain size analysis was carried out to assess the water conductivity of the soil.

UNEP experts taking field measurements at Beit Lahia wastewater treatment plant

Environmental Assessment of the Gaza Strip

Figure 2.   Grain size analysis of sample 05-SOIL-02

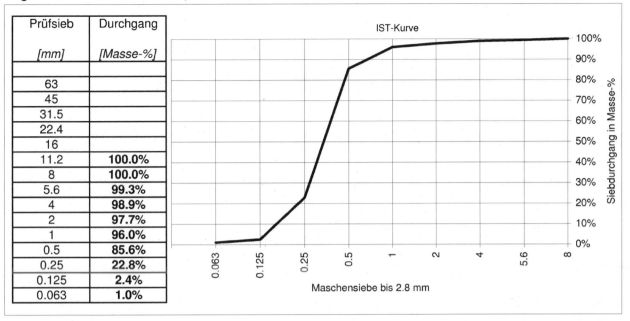

Prüfsieb [mm]	Durchgang [Masse-%]
63	
45	
31.5	
22.4	
16	
11.2	100.0%
8	100.0%
5.6	99.3%
4	98.9%
2	97.7%
1	96.0%
0.5	85.6%
0.25	22.8%
0.125	2.4%
0.063	1.0%

The curve in Figure 2 shows that the grain size of 90 percent of the sample size varies between 0.125 mm and 1.0 mm. According to the grain size analysis results, the hydraulic conductivity is $k_f = 2.6 \times 10^{-4}$ m/s, which is average to high for sand. The underlying soil is highly permeable.

The key issue in the Gaza Strip is that the soil is very favourable for rapid infiltration of the sewage, which is positive from the point of view of the safety of the community living around the lake. However, the high infiltration rate is facilitating rapid contamination of the groundwater. The solution is to avoid the need to have such a holding area by implementing appropriate sewage treatment and disposal options. Once the sewage is drained, the entire area should be reassessed and environmental due diligence carried out before alternative land use can be allowed.

Wadi Gaza (Site no. 15)

Raw sewage from Nussirate, Buraij, Maghazi, Deir El Balah and El-Zahra City is discharged without treatment into Wadi Gaza at a rate of >15,000 m³/ day. The wastewater contaminates the adjacent wetlands, the groundwater and the beaches near the mouth of Wadi Gaza. There is also a notable impact on groundwater quality from infiltration into the aquifer.

To assess the impact on soil in the lower Wadi Gaza area, soil samples were taken from various locations in the flood plains and the beach situated at the wadi mouth. None of the substances analysed was found in concentrations that gave cause for concern. However, disposal of untreated sewage through the open wadi to the sea does have negative impacts since it alters the ecosystem, allows sewage to infiltrate the groundwater and pollutes the sea. The sewage flow into the sea through Wadi Gaza should, therefore, be stopped.

Two aid organizations, Acción Contra El Hambre and Gruppo Volontario Civile, are planning to construct artificial reed beds as an interim measure until the problem can be solved by installing a more sophisticated wastewater treatment plant.[7] While the development of interim measures is understandable, reed beds in this context will not eliminate groundwater contamination completely, and may give a false sense that the problem has been addressed. Issues of sewage treatment and disposal in the Gaza Strip need to be tackled in a systematic way to avoid a catastrophic groundwater situation in the area. This is discussed further in the section on water-related issues below.

UNEP recommends that the disposal of untreated or partially treated effluent into Wadi Gaza should cease as soon as possible. A thorough contamination assessment of the entire Wadi Gaza basin should then be undertaken to see how best the area can be remediated and how the wadi can be restored to its natural functionality. Due to the restricted water flow into the wadi, complete regeneration of the original wadi itself may not be feasible.

Map 10.   Wadi Gaza sewage outfall

Wadi Gaza

Acquisition date: 19/01/2009
Copyright: DigitalGlobe

0   100   200
Meters

Az Zaitoun wastewater treatment plant trickling tower leakage

At the time of the UNEP visit, there was an outflow of water at the rate of approximately 0.5 litres/second (~40 m³/day or 15,000 m³ per annum) from an opening in the trickling tower onto an adjacent waste pile. From the crusts underneath the other openings it could be concluded that water occasionally flowed from these openings as well, raising the observed flow rate even higher. The water accumulated in a puddle on the waste deposited south of the towers, and percolated through it, contaminating the soil and groundwater beneath. It was not possible to observe lateral outflows of landfill leachate, and no samples of this kind were therefore taken. A soil sample was collected close to the site to evaluate the impact of the wastewater outflow. The measured hydraulic conductivity of $k_f = 2.6 \times 10^{-4}$ m/s can be considered high, implying that the landfill leachate infiltrating into the soil from the dump site can be expected to have a severe impact on the groundwater, significantly lowering its quality. An impact can also be expected on drinking water and irrigation wells close to this site.

It is therefore highly recommended to:

- collect water flowing from the trickling towers immediately in order to prevent further leaching of organic and inorganic contaminants from the waste into the groundwater; and

- relocate the waste to a more secure landfill site.

As can be seen from Figure 1,[5] the CMWU is planning to upgrade the Gaza sewage treatment plant in the area of the waste deposits by constructing two more trickling towers (new "bio-towers"). The location chosen for these towers is the waste dump site mentioned previously. However, this is not stable ground and the waste will have to be removed before any construction begins.

Leakage from the Az Zaitoun wastewater treatment plant trickling towers onto an adjacent pile of waste

Other sewage-related contamination

Sewage sludge from the Rafah wastewater treatment plant (08-SOIL-01) was analysed, as well as soil impacted by raw sewage in the Khan Younis storm water infiltration area (11-SOIL-01) (see Table 12).

The sewage sludge from the Rafah wastewater treatment plant contained high levels of zinc, chromium, mercury, copper, lead, and antimony, as could be expected from wastewater sludge. The sludge was within the limit values of the GSSO, but could also be considered Z2 and disposed of in a landfill.

The Khan Younis soil sample was collected at about water level next to the infiltration basin and showed some impact from the wastewater, with respect to zinc, chromium, and mercury. In terms of soil degradation, these concentrations were insignificant, although the sample was taken next to a housing area.

A second sample was taken from the Khan Younis site to evaluate the hydraulic conductivity of the soil in the infiltration area. The curve in Figure 3 shows that the grain size of >70 percent of the sample mass varies between 0.125 mm and 0.25 mm. According to the grain size analysis results, the hydraulic conductivity is $k_f = 1.6 \times 10^{-4}$ m/second, which is considered high. Therefore, the subsoil appears to be appropriate for an infiltration basin.

The key issue here is that the soil is very favourable for rapid infiltration of the sewage, which is positive from the point of view of the safety of the community living around the lake. However, the high infiltration rate is facilitating rapid contamination of the groundwater. As with the Beit Lahia wastewater treatment plant, it is to be expected that due to biological processes at the bottom of the basin, the hydraulic conductivity will decrease, and with equal or increasing effluent quantities, the sewage level in the basin will rise and eventually overflow. In this case, appropriate safety measures should be taken where the overflow could occur. The housing area to the east and southeast is especially vulnerable and is already below the level of the sewage in the basin. In this area, a flood vulnerability analysis is highly recommended, as the sewage lake has grown in recent years.

The solution is to prevent storm water drainage areas from being used as sewage storage areas, as is currently the case. This causes pollution of the groundwater and presents a potential safety hazard to people and a nuisance to the nearby community. An alternative and environmentally sound solution must be found within the overall context of wastewater management in the Gaza Strip, avoiding the need for a holding area of this kind. Once the sewage is drained, the entire area should be reassessed and environmental due diligence carried out before alternative land use can be allowed.

Landfill-related contamination

Solid waste management is also a well recognized environmental problem in the Gaza Strip. Attempts have been made in the past to address this issue and there have been some improvements, but the general situation remains far from satisfactory.

Table 12.   Analysis of Rafah wastewater treatment plant (08-SOIL-01) and Khan Younis storm water infiltration area (11-SOIL-01) samples

Parameter	8-SOIL-01 (mg/kg)	GSSO (mg/kg)	LAGA List (mg/kg)	11-SOIL-01 (mg/kg)	Dutch List (mg/kg)
	Rafah sewage sludge[a]	Limit value	Z value	Khan Younis soil 2-5 cm	Intervention values
Zn	1,140	2,500	Z2 (<1,500)	16.7	720
Cr	79.5	900	Z1 (<180)	15.4	380
Hg	2.92	8	Z2 (<5)	0.01	10
Cu	162	800	Z2 (<400)	<5.0	190
Pb	56.9	900	Z1 (<210)	<10.0	530
As	<5.0	N/A	Z0 (<10)	<5.0	55
Cd	<0.8	10	Z1 (<3)	<0.8	12
Ni	24.8	200	Z1 (<150)	<10.0	210
Sum PAH (EPA)	n.d.	N/A	Z0 (<3)	N/D	40

[a] According to EWC: 19 08 Wastes from wastewater treatment plants not otherwise specified, 19 08 05 sludge from treatment of urban wastewater.
N/A = not applicable
N/D = no data
n.d. = not detected

Environmental Assessment of the Gaza Strip

Figure 3. Grain size analysis of Sample 11-SOIL-02

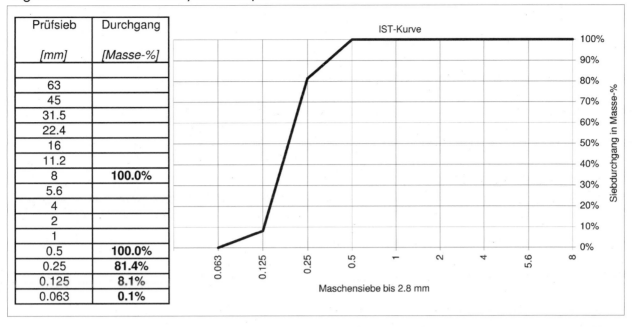

Prüfsieb [mm]	Durchgang [Masse-%]
63	
45	
31.5	
22.4	
16	
11.2	
8	**100.0%**
5.6	
4	
2	
1	
0.5	**100.0%**
0.25	**81.4%**
0.125	**8.1%**
0.063	**0.1%**

Landfill issues include:

- location (too close to communities);

- geology (located over very permeable sand);

- construction (no protective layers below); and

- controls (entry, scavengers, animals, air quality monitoring, etc.).

The recent escalation of hostilities aggravated the situation in several ways. First, the regular collection of waste all but ceased as the movements of people and vehicles were restricted across the Gaza Strip. As a consequence, many municipalities had to resort to measures such as setting fire to accumulated waste or opening new dumpsites, including previously closed landfills, as temporary storage areas. Second, waste could not be segregated as incinerators did not function due to electricity shortages. All landfills thus indiscriminately received hazardous materials such as healthcare waste. Finally, maintenance of existing landfills was severely impaired during the period, and standard practices such as covering and grading could not take place.

If they are improperly managed, landfills can cause contamination through three different transfer paths: air, soil and water.

Air transfer is caused by smoke and soot from landfill fires, as well as by ash and dust from the landfill surface and emissions of gases such as methane and carbon dioxide. Smoke and soot contain high amounts of PAHs, phenols, volatile organics such as benzene, and heavy metals. Except for the volatile components, these substances are also present in the ash blown over the neighbouring territory, and may be found in contaminated dust on the landfills. During the UNEP field visits, fires were visible at some landfills.

Landfill fires are a hazardous aspect of air contamination. They initially cause irritation of the respiratory system and, if they persist, can lead to asphyxiation symptoms, chronic diseases, and cancer. Landfill fires are fed not only by solid fuels such as wood, paper and cardboard in the waste, but also by landfill gas (methane) that is produced under anaerobic conditions inside the landfill itself. Even with no oxygen access, fires may smoulder inside the landfill for months or years. They often create hollow spaces underneath the surface, presenting an additional physical hazard to people and vehicles when they cave in. Outbreaks of gases such as carbon monoxide, methane, and hydrogen sulphide also represent a hazard for people working on such sites. Carbon monoxide and hydrogen sulphide can lead to asphyxiation symptoms while methane can lead to deflagration.

Map 11.   Solid waste dumping sites in Gaza

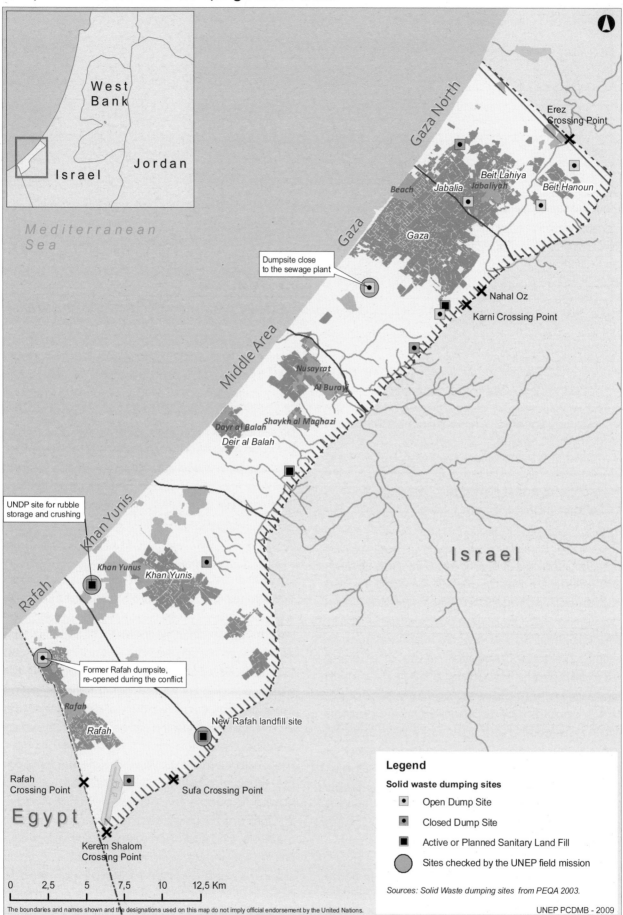

West
Bank

Jordan

Israel

Mediterranean
Sea

Gaza North

Erez
Crossing Point

Beit Lahiya

Beach
Jabalia   Jabaliyah

Beit Hanoun

Gaza

Gaza

Dumpsite close
to the sewage plant

Nahal Oz

Karni Crossing Point

Middle Area

Nusayrat

Al Buraij

Shaykh al Maghazi

Dayr al Balah

Deir al Balah

Khan Yunis

UNDP site for rubble
storage and crushing

Israel

Rafah

Khan Yunus

Khan Yunis

Former Rafah dumpsite,
re-opened during the conflict

Rafah

Rafah

New Rafah landfill site

Rafah
Crossing Point

Sufa Crossing Point

Egypt

Kerem Shalom
Crossing Point

Legend

Solid waste dumping sites

- Open Dump Site
- Closed Dump Site
- Active or Planned Sanitary Land Fill
- Sites checked by the UNEP field mission

Sources: Solid Waste dumping sites from PEQA 2003.

UNEP PCDMB - 2009

0   2,5   5   7,5   10   12,5 Km

The boundaries and names shown and the designations used on this map do not imply official endorsement by the United Nations.

Environmental Assessment of the Gaza Strip

Groundwater and surface water bodies are often affected by landfill leachate which is generated from the humidity of the waste itself and from rainwater percolating through the waste. On its way through the waste, the water leaches heavy metals and other organic and inorganic substances. The organic and inorganic load of leachate can be extremely high and depends on the development stage of the landfill. Usually, landfill leachate collects at the bottom of landfills as well as in surrounding drainage structures and open water bodies. Upon entering a natural ecosystem, it causes water quality to deteriorate quickly, as free oxygen in the water is consumed by the leachate's high COD and BOD. Water organisms relying on free oxygen in water die off, and without remediation measures, the ecosystem can be seriously affected (see Table 13).

Leachate may enter the ground if the landfill is unlined and permeability allows it. In well designed landfills, this transfer path is interrupted by either positioning a landfill in an area with low water permeability of the soil (e.g. clay) or by constructing a landfill with a base lining. In addition, leachate collection systems leading to treatment systems are constructed underneath the landfill.

No base lining or leachate control systems were found in the landfill sites visited in the Gaza Strip. Leachate was observed on some sites, such as in the Rafah landfill. In these cases, the risk of groundwater contamination is only limited by soil permeability and desiccation, and the soil's ability to absorb contaminants. The soil pathway in landfill areas usually affects outflows of landfill leachate on neighbouring land. These effects are usually very limited and restricted to a few thousand square metres immediately around the landfill. The soil contamination in this case depends on the organic and inorganic contaminants in the leachate, which may vary widely. However, over a period of time, the leachate can reach and pollute the groundwater.

Landfill leachate leaking from Rafah landfill

Rafah landfill site (Site no. 25)

The Rafah landfill is situated in the southeast of the Gaza Strip, approximately 5 km northeast of the former Gaza Airport and 800 metres from the Israeli border wall. The landfill covers an area of approximately 33,000 m³ (3.3 hectares or 33 dunums). The waste is not compacted and reaches a height of approximately 15-20 m above ground level. The landfill does not have a base lining, leachate control, or landfill gas collection systems. The nearest inhabited house is approximately 20 metres away, and larger settlements lie at a distance of about 800-1,500 metres.

Table 13.   Typical concentrations of landfill leachate

Component (unit)	Acidic phase, 0-2 years		Methanogenic phase, >2 years
	Low	High	Average
pH (-)	5	6.5	7.5
COD (mg/litre)	20,000	40,000	2,200
BOD5 (mg/litre)	10,000	30,000	400

Leachate traces were observed on top of, at the side of and underneath the landfill. The water from the leachate appeared to evaporate quickly if exposed to the arid climate. Underneath the landfill, the leachate could actually enter the soil and subsequently the groundwater. Even though precipitation in this area (at 225 mm per annum) is low and evapo-transpiration is high, leachate collection should be implemented at all sites considering the already precarious condition of the groundwater.

Samples were taken from soil on top of the landfill contaminated with leachate (25-SOIL-01); soil for grain size and chemical analysis from 1.2-1.4

metres below the landfill base (25-SOIL-02); landfill ash from approximately 2 metres above the landfill base (25-SOIL-03); soil from 5 metres away from the landfill base (25-SOIL-04); and soil from 1.4-1.5 metres below the landfill base (25-SOIL-05). Table 14 lists the parameters of the soil analysis.

Table 14 shows that the highest heavy metal and PAH concentrations were found in the landfill ash, which resulted from incineration of waste. The comparison of the waste ash with the LAGA List shows that most of the parameters analysed comply with Z0 and Z1, except for copper (Z2). Restricted backfill under controlled conditions is therefore recommended.

Table 14.   Analysis of Rafah landfill samples

Parameter	25 SOIL 03 (mg/kg)	LAGA List (mg/kg)	25 SOIL 01 (mg/kg)	25 SOIL 04 (mg/kg)	25 SOIL 02 (mg/kg)	25 SOIL 05 (mg/kg)	Dutch List (mg/kg)
	Landfill ash[a]	Z value	Soil, top of landfill	0-0.05 m below basis	1.2-1.4 m below basis	1.4-1.5 m below basis	Intervention value
Sb	10.9	N/A	<1.0	<1.0	<1.0	<1.0	15
As	<5.0	Z0 (<10)	<5.0	<5.0	<5.0	<5.0	55
Pb	111	Z1 (<210)	13.4	13.1	<10.0	<10.0	530
Cd	2.2	Z1 (<3)	<0.8	<0.8	<0.8	<0.8	12
Cr	30.9	Z1 (<180)	29.6	39.5	27.5	38.6	380
Cu	232	Z 2 (<400)	14.5	15	<5.0	7.7	190
Ni	23.5	Z1 (<150)	16.4	27.6	18.6	21.9	210
Hg	0.06	Z0 (<0.1)	<0.01	<0.01	<0.01	<0.01	10
Zn	377	Z1 (<450)	47.2	51.3	29.3	38.1	720
Methylene-3,4-phenol	N/D	N/A	0.2	N/D	N/D	N/D	40[b]
Phenol	N/D	N/A	0.2	N/D	N/D	N/D	
p,p'-DDD	N/D	N/A	0.0017	N/D	N/D	N/D	4[c]
p,p'-DDE	N/D	N/A	0.0027	N/D	N/D	N/D	
o,p'-DDT	N/D	N/A	<0.001	N/D	N/D	N/D	
p,p'-DDT	N/D	N/A	<0.001	N/D	N/D	N/D	
Phenanthren	0.48	N/A	<0.05	<0.05	<0.05	<0.05	N/A
Anthracen	0.06	N/A	<0.05	<0.05	<0.05	<0.05	N/A
Fluoranthen	0.12	N/A	<0.05	<0.05	<0.05	<0.05	N/A
Pyren	0.11	N/A	<0.05	<0.05	<0.05	<0.05	N/A
Chrysen	0.08	N/A	<0.05	<0.05	<0.05	<0.05	N/A
Benzo(a)anthracen	0.07	N/A	<0.05	<0.05	<0.05	<0.05	N/A
Benzo(a)pyren	0.12	Z0 (<0.3)	<0.05	<0.05	<0.05	<0.05	N/A
Sum PAH (EPA)	1.03	Z0 (<3)	<0.50	<0.50	<0.50	<0.50	40

[a] Dutch List does not apply to waste, according to EWC: 19 01 Wastes from incineration or pyrolysis of waste, 19 01 99 Wastes not otherwise specified.
[b] sum of phenols
[c] sum of DDT/DDE/DDD
N/A = not applicable
N/D = no data

Environmental Assessment of the Gaza Strip

Soil contaminated by leachate and the soil sampled below the landfill contains contaminants, but these are below the intervention values of the Dutch List, indicating a somewhat low mobility of contaminants. The occurrence of DDD and DDE as degradation products of DDT on top of the landfill in leachate-contaminated soil may be an indication that contaminated soil has been deposited on the landfill. The absence of the original substance DDT at a detection limit of 0.001 mg/kg is a sign that no DDT was deposited on the landfill.

To evaluate the permeability of the soil under the landfill site, a larger sample (25-SOIL-02/Viatec 5771-3) was taken to carry out a grain size analysis.

The curve in Figure 4 shows that the grain size of 90 percent of the sample mass varies between 0.063 mm and 0.5 mm. According to the grain size analysis results, the hydraulic conductivity is $k_f = 4.6 \times 10^{-5}$ m/second, which is average for a silty sand. In combination with the low precipitation and high evapo-transpiration in the Rafah area, this may be sufficient to reduce the impact of the landfill on the groundwater. However, if there are cracks present, they will facilitate direct percolation of highly concentrated leachate into the groundwater.

In any case, the slope of the landfill should be diminished to minimize the risk of slope failure. In addition, the slope should be covered with silty sand and/or clay to minimize infiltration of precipitation. In daily operations, the waste should be compacted as a measure against vectors and to minimize pore volume.

Base of the Rafah landfill

Figure 4.   Grain size analysis of sample 25-SOIL-02, 1.4-1.5m below landfill base

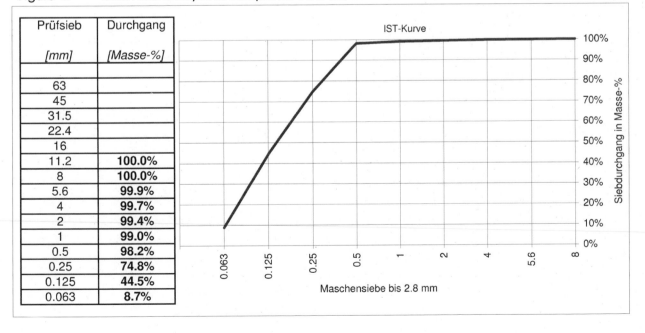

Prüfsieb [mm]	Durchgang [Masse-%]
63	
45	
31.5	
22.4	
16	
11.2	100.0%
8	100.0%
5.6	99.9%
4	99.7%
2	99.4%
1	99.0%
0.5	98.2%
0.25	74.8%
0.125	44.5%
0.063	8.7%

Waste dump site at the Az Zaitoun wastewater treatment plant (Site no. 17)

The waste dump site at the Az Zaitoun or Gaza City wastewater treatment plant, discussed in the section on sewage-related contamination above, is a critical example of waste management in the Gaza Strip. The plant is approximately 1 km south of Gaza City and comprises seven basins, two trickling filter towers and an administrative building. Close to the trickling filter towers in the southeast of the plant there is a waste dump site of approximately 15,000 m² in area and 3 metres in height, or approximately 45,000 m³ in volume. The waste consists of municipal solid waste, mixed with asbestos and dried wastewater sludge. In addition, it is infiltrated by wastewater from the adjacent trickling towers, as described above.

In this area, groundwater reserves are stressed by high demand, so groundwater protection should be a priority. Although the annual rainfall is only about 400 mm, this site requires urgent action. The site should be closed, and the contents removed to a properly located and designed landfill site. Once due diligence has been carried out, the site should be restored.

Wadi Gaza dump site (Site no. 15)

Wadi Gaza, also discussed in the section on sewage-related contamination above, is the outflow of a drainage area of approximately 3,500 km² that drains parts of the Hebron Mountains and Northern Negev Heights. The wadi's ecological importance arises from the fact that it is the Gaza Strip's main natural feature and only natural open body of water, besides being an important landmark and resting point for migratory bird species in the spring and autumn. The mouth of Wadi Gaza used to be home to a salt marsh ecosystem that largely disappeared during the construction of the coastal road bridge in the first half of the 1990s. Wadi Gaza was declared a nature reserve in 2002, and a Wadi Gaza Nature Park project was initiated.[8] For a number of reasons, however, this conservation initiative did not achieve its goals.[9]

Several attempts have been made to integrate Wadi Gaza into international protection programmes such as those developed under the 1991 Ramsar agreement, but they have not been successful to date. Wadi Gaza continues to be used as a waste dump site along its course. The UNEP team visited the area around the wadi mouth, where approximately

Wadi Gaza waste dump site

20,000 m² is used as a waste dump site. The waste itself is being used for land reclamation, and the bed of the stream is being filled with it. Taking into account a waste height of 1-2 metres, an estimated 20,000-40,000 m³ of waste has been deposited in this area so far. It was not possible to determine whether the recent hostilities had led to an increase in waste dumped at this site.

As the water from the wadi percolates through the waste according to the rise and fall of the groundwater table, contaminants are leached from the waste into the water and subsequently into the sea, constituting an additional source of contamination. The proportion of contamination from waste, however, appears to be insignificant compared to the load imposed on the wadi by raw sewage.

Chemical analysis of the water flowing through Wadi Gaza indicated anoxic conditions showing high ammonia content. Organic parameters are high: benzene, toluene, ethyl benzene and xylene could be measured – mainly toluene – and the faecal bacteria concentration was extremely high (see details in the section on sewage above).

As sewage-related contamination and waste deposition on this site could not be reliably distinguished, the soil samples taken from this site are discussed in the section on sewage. Considering the ecological value of Wadi Gaza, waste dumping should be stopped immediately. The removal of waste inhibiting the flow of water into the wadi should also be considered, although this is a secondary issue compared to the urgency of the sewage problem.

Map 12. Waste dump site at the Gaza wastewater treatment plant

Waste dump site

Sewage basins

Acquisition date: 06/06/2005
Copyright: GeoEye

Extension of waste dump site

Acquisition date: 19/01/2009
Copyright: DigitalGlobe

0   100   200
Meters

Map 13.   Tal El Sultan old landfill site

Water treatment plant in construction

Housing area

Acquisition date: 21/01/2009
Copyright: GeoEye

Partially vegetated part of the abandoned dumping site

Re-opened during the conflict

Tal El Sultan old landfill site (Site no. 8)

The old landfill site of Tal El Sultan lies next to the Egyptian border on the north-western Rafah city limit. The nearest houses are less than 50 metres away. The site covers an area of approximately 60,000 m² (6 hectares or 60 dunums). The site had been closed upon the opening of the Rafah landfill (Site no. 25), but was used during and after the recent escalation of violence as a temporary storage site and transfer station for municipal solid waste. The site has no landfill gas collection, leachate control system or base lining.

During the visit, the UNEP team observed scavenging by adults and children. There was no compaction, separation or covering of the waste. The municipal solid waste on the landfill also contained openly deposited healthcare waste (e.g. sharps and needles) and slaughterhouse waste (feathers, bones, etc.). Both of these constitute a health hazard.

According to information provided by UNDP/PAPP, the landfill is supposed to be closed and should not be used after the waste accumulated during and shortly after the recent hostilities has been removed. At the time of the visit in May 2009, however, the site was still being used. The site itself constitutes a health hazard to people working on and near it, as well as to the neighbouring community. The slaughterhouse waste is a particular problem, as it attracts rats, which may transmit diseases such as leptospirosis, salmonellosis, meningitis, and rat bite fever. Other disease vectors in the area are sand flies (*Phlebotomus sp.*) that lay eggs in places rich in organic matter and transmit leishmaniasis, and common flies.

The site should be closed and its contents removed to a properly located and designed landfill site. After due diligence has been carried out, the site should be restored.

Scavenger on the Tal El Sultan old landfill site

The decommissioned Tal El Sultan landfill site was reopened during the recent hostilities

Hazardous healthcare waste in a Gaza City hospital container

Hazardous healthcare waste (HHCW)

WHO defines HHCW as "waste generated by hospitals, laboratories, doctors' surgeries and any other facility where health services to humans or animals are delivered." On average, HHCW consists of 80 percent domestic waste, 16.4 percent infectious/pathogenic waste, 1.1 percent blood and body fluids and <1 percent other (e.g. radioactive or chemical waste). WHO has suggested, as an indicative figure, an average value of 3 kg per hospital bed/day for the generation of HHCW.

According to the WHO,[10] 1,380 Palestinians were killed and more than 50,000 injured during the December 2008 – January 2009 hostilities. First aid and treatment of victims are the main source of hazardous materials (potentially infectious, bio-contaminated material, blood, etc.) in healthcare centres during crises like the one that occurred in the Gaza Strip.

Also according to the WHO,[11] there are some 2,100 hospital beds in the Gaza Strip which would be expected to have generated some 60 tonnes of waste during the 22 days of the conflict. This would include approximately 48 tonnes of municipal solid waste, 10 tonnes of infectious/pathogenic waste and 2 tonnes of hazardous waste made up of blood, body fluids, etc. As noted above, incinerators did not function during the hostilities, and HHCW could not be transported even to regular landfills, as municipal collection services had collapsed.

Much of the backlog has now been cleared through incineration and disposal to landfills. Indeed, visits to landfills revealed evidence of HHCW in the waste stream. At nearly every site, sharps, needles, bandages, and other related materials were found. In all cases, the waste was not disposed of in separate areas, or in marked or specially coloured plastic bags, but was openly accessible.

Management of HHCW is a serious environmental issue in the Gaza Strip that pre-dates the recent escalation of hostilities. Although the problem was exacerbated during this period, the management challenge itself needs to be addressed in the long term.

Water-related issues

Pressure on water resources in the Gaza Strip

Water resources in the Gaza Strip were already in the throes of an environmental crisis prior to the latest escalation of hostilities. However, the recent events aggravated the situation in several ways. First, the collapse of sewage treatment during the period accelerated the pollution load into the underlying aquifer. Second, the lack of reliable and sufficient drinking water supply during the fighting meant that the population used whatever water it had access to, irrespective of its supply source. Third, even water supplied through municipal systems and private tankers was both untreated and untested, leaving the population exposed to contamination.

The Gaza Strip covers an area of 378 square kilometres, which is underlain by an unconfined aquifer contained in sandstone. This aquifer, known as the coastal aquifer, is a continuum from Egypt through the Gaza Strip to Israel. Historically, the aquifer had high quality freshwater and was shallow, which facilitated the development of agriculture and the growth of civilization in the area. The aquifer is overlaid by soil of high permeability, including sand dunes. This means that rain easily enters and recharges the aquifer. The area receives an average rainfall of 300 mm per year and it is estimated that

up to 46 percent of the rain that falls on the Gaza Strip goes on to recharge the aquifer. This net positive balance of water inflow used to ensure that the aquifer did not experience salt water intrusion.

However, political changes in the region caused dramatic demographic changes in the Gaza Strip as of 1948, and by 1967, the Gaza Strip had become a net consumer of the aquifer. The political developments of 1967 and the situation that followed presented additional challenges to water resources in the Gaza Strip. The Israeli settlements that were established in the area were primarily agriculture-based and by the 1990s, were reported to extract about 3 million cubic metres of water per year (92 percent for agriculture). The steady drop in water levels and increasing salinity has been evident in the Gaza Strip ever since. Even though the water deficit challenge in the Gaza Strip has been well studied for several decades, no solution has yet been implemented and the situation in the Gaza Strip continues to deteriorate.

It is estimated that the annual recharge from rainfall in the Gaza Strip to the coastal aquifer is about 45 million cubic metres. Abstraction has been well in excess of sustainable levels: indeed the most recent estimate of abstraction, dating from 2007, is about 163 million cubic metres per year (CMWU, 2008). The consequence is that water

Figure 5. Schematic structure of aquifers in the Gaza Strip (Source: Dan, Greitzer 1967)

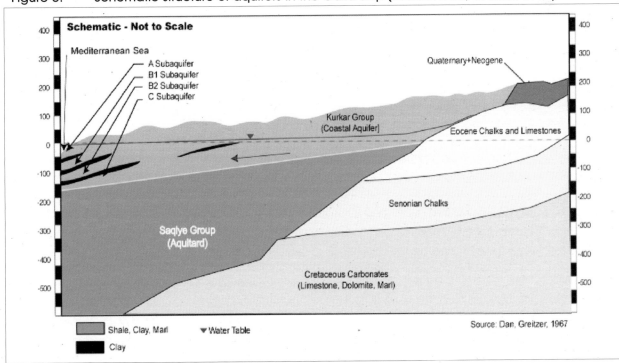

Figure 6.   Groundwater pollution in the Gaza Strip (schematic)

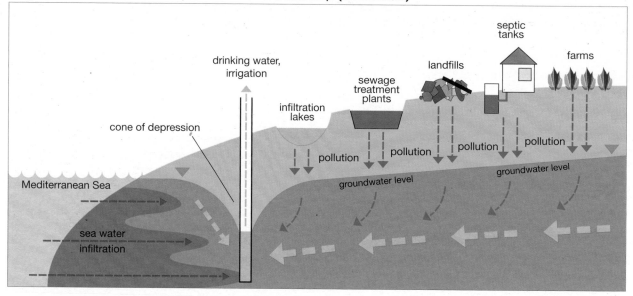

levels are declining in areas where abstraction is greatest, while salt water infiltration from the sea is causing the aquifer to become more saline. The salinity levels in most parts of the Gaza Strip are now above the WHO approved guideline of 250 mg/litre, and often much higher.

Water quality issues

While the coastal aquifer has been under pressure from over-abstraction, it has also been subjected to extremely high loads of contamination from the percolation of sewage and irrigation water. Before 1990, organized sewage systems were not common in the Gaza Strip and households depended largely on septic tanks for sanitation. Due to the high permeability of the topsoil, the overflow water from the septic tanks infiltrated the groundwater directly. Since the septic tank system does not treat the sewage, the infiltrated water contained both bacterial and chemical contamination.

In the 1990s, sewage collection was centralized and a number of sewage treatment plants were planned in the Gaza Strip. Four of these facilities were built, but they are not effective as most have large open ponds that are either unlined or improperly lined, so that concentrated sewage leaks into the groundwater, causing acute pollution.

Groundwater is also polluted in another way. As part of the effort to accelerate recharge of the aquifer, large infiltration basins were created. The idea was that storm water and sewage water would be collected

separately. Sewage would be sent for treatment to the sewage treatment facilities, and storm water would be recharged from these ponds. The location and design of these ponds was intended to facilitate easy and quick recharge. However, whenever the sewage pumps fail, the infiltration ponds become convenient dumping grounds for raw sewage. The net effect is that raw sewage infiltrates into the groundwater.

The pollution of groundwater is contributing to two main types of water contamination in the Gaza Strip. First, and most importantly, it is causing the nitrate levels in the groundwater to increase. In most parts of the Gaza Strip, especially around areas of intensive sewage infiltration, the nitrate level in groundwater is far above the WHO accepted guideline of 50 mg/litre as nitrates (see Palestinian Water Authority, 2002). Second, because the water abstracted now is high in salt, the sewage is also very saline and hence infiltrating sewage only adds to the salinity of the aquifer.

It has been well known and well documented for decades that higher levels of nitrates in drinking water can induce methemoglobinaemia in young children. This is because babies up to six months old, who depend mainly on lactation for their nutrients, have alkaline intestinal tracts that are conducive to the oxidation of haemoglobin to methemoglobin. As the children develop, their intestines become more acidic and the microenvironment within the intestine is no longer conducive to the formation of methemoglobin. The incidence of methemoglobinaemia in infants in the Gaza Strip is extremely high (see Box 2).

Environmental Assessment of the Gaza Strip

Box 2. Blue babies in the Gaza Strip

Methemoglobinaemia is a blood disorder characterized by higher than normal levels of methemoglobin, a form of haemoglobin that does not bind oxygen. When haemoglobin is oxidized it becomes methemoglobin, its structure changes and it is no longer able to bind oxygen or deliver it to the tissues, and anaemia can result. This state is referred to as methemoglobinaemia.

Infants suffering from methemoglobinaemia may appear otherwise healthy but exhibit intermittent signs of blueness around the mouth, hands and feet. They may have episodes of breathing trouble, diarrhoea and vomiting. In some cases, infants with methemoglobinaemia have a peculiar lavender colour but show little distress. Blood samples appear chocolate brown and do not turn pink when exposed to air. When the methemoglobin level is high, infants express a marked lethargy, excessive salivation and loss of consciousness. Convulsions and death can occur when methemoglobin levels are extremely high.

Reduced oxygen transport capacity becomes clinically manifest when methemoglobin concentrations in the blood surpass 10 percent of the hemoglobin concentrations. The normal level of methemoglobin in the blood of adults is <2 percent; of infants under three months of age <3 percent (WHO, 2007).

WHO established a guideline values for nitrates already in 1958. The 1993 guidelines concluded that extensive epidemiological studies supported the guideline value for nitrate at 10 mg/litre (as nitrogen) but that the value should be expressed as nitrates as this is the chemical entity that concerns public health. The current (WHO 2008) guideline value for nitrate is 50 mg/litre.

A disturbing feature of nitrate as a contaminant is that it is colourless, tasteless and odourless. This, and the fact that the population has not been warned about it, means that people will continue to consume drinking water with high nitrates unless they are informed about it.

Monitoring of groundwater in the Gaza Strip indicated the presence of nitrates as early as the 1990s. It emerged that the elevated levels of nitrate were primarily caused by the infiltration of sewage from domestic septic tanks as well as agricultural runoff into the groundwater. Nitrate values in the Gaza Strip have continued to rise and currently present a health risk throughout the territory. Since the aquifer is a continuum and pollution is occurring across the Gaza Strip, albeit in varying degrees, it is not surprising that high levels of nitrate are found throughout the Gaza Strip (see Figure 9).

In the 1990s, data began to emerge about the incidence of blue babies in the Gaza Strip. A 1998 survey (Al Absi 2008) studied 640 blood samples from children in paediatric hospitals across the Gaza Strip. The presence of 10 percent methemoglobin was taken as the minimum level indicating methemoglobinaemia. The study showed that the prevalence of methemoglobinaemia – or "blue babies" – in the Gaza Strip, according to this criterion, is 48 percent.

In a more recent study (Abu Naser et al. 2007), 338 babies under one year old who attended 12 primary health centres for vaccination were tested for methemoglobins between June 2002 and November 2002. The study group was 53.3 percent male and 46.7 percent female; the mean age of the group was 4.5 months. The main source of water that they consumed was tap water from groundwater (59.5 percent) followed by treated water (20.4 percent), home filtered water (11.2 percent). The rest used private wells. The proportion of children with methemoglobin higher than 5 percent was 48.5 percent.

The current status of methemoglobinaemia in the Gaza Strip is unknown as there are no systematic studies available in the public domain. However, as mentioned previously, nitrate levels in the groundwater have increased and nitrates are more widespread in the area. Consequently, it can be expected that the problem is still prevalent in the Gaza Strip, and in the absence of widespread awareness, a large number of children are at risk.

The following actions are proposed to address this challenge.

- **Provide safe water for infants**: There is enough evidence to suggest that some children in the Gaza Strip are at risk of consuming water with elevated levels of nitrates, leading to methemoglobinaemia. Immediate action should be taken to provide all children under one year old with adequate clean, safe water.

- **A study on the prevalence of methemoglobinaemia**: Due to the reported prevalence of methemoglobinaemia in the Gaza Strip, a comprehensive study should be undertaken. WHO, UNEP, the United Nations Children's Fund (UNICEF) and UNRWA can provide technical support for such a study.

Figure 7. Groundwater level declination in well (P/61) (Source: PWA 2002)

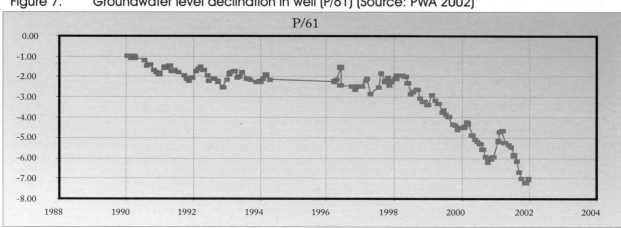

Figure 8. Salinity increase in well (L/86) (Source: PWA 2002)

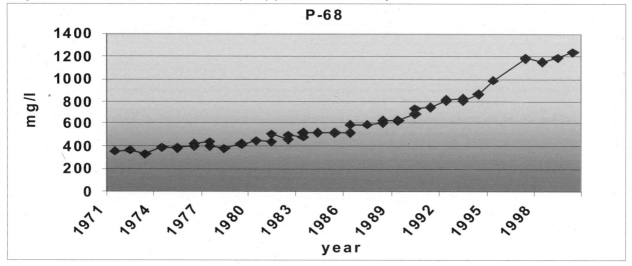

Figure 9. Nitrate in the groundwater of the Gaza Strip (Source: PWA 2002)

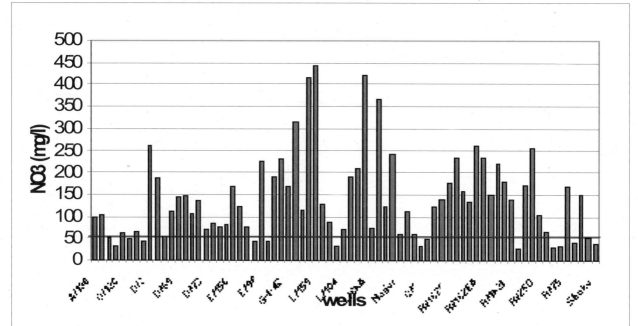

Environmental Assessment of the Gaza Strip

Map 14. Sewage in storm water recharge pond

Acquisition date: 06/2005
Copyright: DigitalGlobe

Acquisition date: 14/06/2007
Copyright: DigitalGlobe

Greenhouses

Sewage filled in storm
water recharge pond

Housing

Cultivated area

0   200   400
                Meters

Acquisition date: 21/01/2009
Copyright: DigitalGlobe

Changing salinity of irrigation water might render traditional farming knowledge insufficient

Though it is evident that the stress on groundwater resources in the Gaza Strip was aggravated by the increased load of sewage pollution that was generated during the recent hostilities, it is not possible scientifically to differentiate between the existing pollution of the aquifer and any pollution added by the recent events. It will also take some time before the pollution from this period spreads into the aquifer. The UNEP assessment therefore, did not attempt to distinguish between the pollution caused by recent hostilities and prior existing contamination. Instead, samples of water from various sources of drinking and irrigation supplies in the Gaza Strip were taken to confirm reported elevations of salts and nitrates.

Private wells

There are a number of private wells in the Gaza Strip, only some of which are officially registered. As much as 60-65 percent of total water use is for agriculture, due to historical, social, and economic reasons. Many people in the Gaza Strip depend on agriculture as a source of income, and large areas

of land have been reclaimed for agriculture over the past few decades, especially during the Egyptian mandate on the Gaza Strip that ended in 1967. This expansion of agricultural areas has involved the drilling of as many as 4,000 agricultural wells. And because of the difficult political and economic conditions of recent years in the Gaza Strip, people have become more and more dependent on agriculture, resulting in additional, random wells being drilled without permission from the authorities. As many as 2,000 wells are estimated to have been drilled in this way, and they have of course led to further discharge, which has contributed to more rapid deterioration of the aquifer.

It has been observed that the users of private wells are usually very disciplined, and that water is not wasted but rather seen as "private gold." The water extracted in this way is mainly used in agriculture and only in small volumes for drinking, though the possibility of this water being used routinely for drinking – in particular when municipal water supply

Environmental Assessment of the Gaza Strip

systems collapse – cannot be ruled out. Water is usually not sold to other families.

Water from nine private wells was analysed in detail and both nitrate and chloride values are reproduced in Table 15.

The samples confirmed the regional differences in salt and nitrate concentrations:

- The nitrate concentrations were measured up to 331 mg NO$_3$/litre, as compared to the WHO guideline of 50 mg/litre as nitrates.

- The chloride concentrations measured between 141 and 1,840 mg/litre. All but two samples exceeded the WHO guideline of 250 mg/litre as chloride.

Table 15.   Water quality analysis from water wells in the Gaza Strip

WHO guidelines	Chemical concentration		
	Chloride (mg/l)	Nitrate (mg/l)	Conductivity (µS/cm)
	250	50	
Sample reference			
1 water 01	760	45.2	3,620
4 water 01	220	46.9	1,430
5 water 02	250	27.9	1,620
11 water 02	658	52	3,140
13 water 01	538	331	3,190
17 water 02	625	1.4	3,590
29 water 01	141	<1	1,510
Al Deira Water	1,840	121	6,550
Satar 001	354	40.5	2,160

Private well drilling operation in northern Gaza Strip

Drinking water supply

A number of wells feed the drinking water supply networks. As mentioned above, the five Governorates in the Gaza Strip and the 25 municipalities are responsible for the water supply for domestic use under the umbrella of the CMWU. The Palestinian Water Authority (PWA) is the regulatory body for the water sector in terms of environment, quality and economics.

Three municipal drinking waters were analysed in detail (see Table 16).

As can be seen from Table 16, none of these sources fully meet the WHO guidelines on drinking water quality when both chloride and nitrate concentrations are considered. In one well, nitrate is as high as 297 mg/litre. The water from the pumping station for UNRWA is currently safe from nitrate and the only concern is chloride causing a salty taste. However, the challenge is clear: there are fewer and fewer places in the Gaza Strip where groundwater can be pumped directly and used as a source of safe drinking water.

Tankered water

One tankered water sample was taken on a street in Rafah town. Steel distribution tanks like the one the sample came from were observed all over the Gaza Strip. The analysis indicated good quality water that met WHO guidelines for drinking water. The chloride concentration was measured at 26 mg Cl/litre and the nitrate at 29 mg NO_3/litre.

Bottled water

One bottled water/mineral water sample (Al Safa) was sent to the laboratory for detailed analysis. The water fulfilled the WHO guideline values for drinking water: the chloride concentration was measured at 47 mg Cl/litre and the nitrate at 38 mg NO_3/litre. Surprisingly, the water contained volatile organic compounds (VOCs) (measured according to EPA 524.2) – chloroform, tetrachloroethylene, dibromochloromethane and bromoform in the low microgramme per litre range. How these organic compounds came to be in the water is a matter of speculation, but even in low concentrations, the presence of VOCs in bottled water is undesirable. In this case, the VOCs probably originated from the bottles used, since such bottles are often produced in plastic recycling facilities with poor quality control.

UNEP experts sampling drinking water

Table 16.   Water quality analysis of drinking water sources

WHO guidelines	Chemical concentration		
	Chloride (mg/l)	Nitrate (mg/l)	Conductivity (µS/cm)
	250	50	
Sample reference			
6 water 01	584	98.1	2,390
10 water 01	414	297	2,370
Central Water 01	488	25.1	2,040

Environmental Assessment of the Gaza Strip

Marine and coastal rapid assessment

The Gaza coastline has been subjected to sewage pollution, waste dumping and over-fishing for many decades, but the situation was aggravated when sewage treatment systems collapsed during the recent hostilities, leading to the daily deposition of tens of thousands of cubic metres of raw sewage into the Mediterranean Sea.

The Gaza littoral environment consists of a coastline of about 40 km in length, made up of sandy beaches with occasional sandstone outcrops. The coast is open, without any islands or major reef areas. With the exception of the shallow area off Rafah in the south, the shelf slopes gently from the shore to about 100 metres in depth ten nautical miles off the coast.

A northbound coastal counter-clockwise current dominates the coastal zone and offshore areas of the eastern Mediterranean. Until the completion of the Aswan Dam in 1966, the coastal and marine environment of the naturally oligotrophic Levantine Basin was highly influenced by the sediments and freshwater originating from the Nile River. Through millennia, the northbound current resulting in long-shore transportation of sediments and brackish water along the coast shaped the coastal zone of present-day Egypt, the Gaza Strip and Israel. The sediment transportation and the corresponding input of nutrients have decreased very significantly since 1966, with dramatic ecological consequences in the form of reduced stocks of fish and shellfish.

All the beaches and coastal areas of the Gaza Strip have been affected by human activity to some extent. Particularly in places where houses and other facilities have been established near the beach or on the sand dunes between the coastal road and the sea, erosion and degradation of the coastal vegetation is clearly visible. In addition, sand mining on the coastal dunes can be observed in many places. This practice is likely to contribute to the increasing coastal erosion. In the area known as Gaza beaches, where coastal erosion has been extensive, a sea wall has been constructed by depositing boulders along the upper beach, to protect against wave erosion.

Prolific algae growth due to sewage outflow into the Mediterranean Sea

UNEP experts sampling seawater

A number of small sewage outlets can be found along the Gaza coastline, either in the form of pipes or of open sewers that empty onto the beach. Larger sewage pipes releasing more significant volumes (in the range of one to several cubic metres per second) are located in the south in Rafah and El Nuseirat. Other outlets are located, for example, in Deir El Balah Refugee Camp, Shati, Gaza City and Beit Lahia. The outlets in Rafah and El Nuseirat release partly treated sewage. Wadi Gaza is also causing pollution to the coastal waters from untreated sewage. From the flourishing growth of green algae along the coastline, it is obvious that the coastal zone is subjected to eutrophication.

UNEP collected eight samples from the sea that were analysed for a range of parameters. Table 17 shows the results of the analysis, revealing very high concentrations of *Escherichia coli* and *Enterococci*.

As expected, the pollution of coastal waters by sewage is severe in areas near point sources. Here, levels of *Enterococci* are far above the WHO standards for recreational water and are clearly a threat to human health. Although most of the Gaza Strip's beaches are impacted by sewage pollution and warnings are periodically issued by the relevant authorities, they are still extensively used by local families for recreation purposes, as virtually no alternatives are available.

Table 17.   Bacteriological contamination of seawater in Gaza

WHO guideline for recreational water	Concentration of biological pollutants	
	E. coli (cfu/100 ml)	Enterococci (cfu/100 ml)
		100
Sample reference		
18 water 001	20	560
18 water 002	10	170
19 water 001	10	20
21 water 002	14,000	1,260
28 water 002	10	10
30 water 001	10	220
31 water 001	70	176
32 water 001	10	100

Four samples of fish and one sample of mussels were analysed. Three of the fish samples were purchased at the fish market in Gaza City and one was bought from a fisherman who had been fishing at the entrance of the Gaza harbour. The mussels were collected from rocks at the beach at Al Soudani north of Gaza City.

The samples were prepared, extracted and analysed at the GBA Fruit Analytic GMBH laboratory in Sweden according to the method DFG S19, which analyses for the presence of several hundred organochlorine pesticides, organophosphates, pyrethroides and other nitrogen-containing compounds, triazines, triazoles and strobilurines. In order to identify the individual substances, a mass-spectrum library was used. In addition, a semi-quantitative determination could be conducted, as internal and external standards were used.

Map 15.   Seawater sampling sites

West
Bank

Jordan

Israel

*Mediterranean
Sea*

Gaza North

Erez
Crossing Point

18

19

32

31

21

15

30

Beit Lahiya

Beit Hanoun

Jabalia

Gaza

Gaza

Nahal Oz

Karni Crossing Point

Middle Area

Deir al Balah

Israel

Khan Yunis

Khan Yunis

Rafah

28

Rafah

Rafah
Crossing Point

Sufa Crossing Point

Egypt

Kerem Shalom
Crossing Point

0   2   4   6   8   10 Km

The boundaries and names shown and the designations used on this map do not imply official endorsement by the United Nations.

Legend

▲   Sea water samples

Source: UNEP, Field Mission 2009.

UNEP PCDMB - 2009

Only a few pesticides could be detected in the samples that were collected. All the samples contained p,p-DDE, a break-down product of DDT. This indicates that DDT is in use in Gaza or neighbouring areas. In addition to the presence of DDE, one of the samples – juvenile snappers caught by fishermen directly outside the Gaza harbour – also showed presence of p,p-DDD, p,p-DDT and o,p-DDT. This further strengthens the theory that DDT is in use in Gaza itself, as these were juvenile fishes caught very close to Gaza City (see Table 18).

Furthermore, all samples contained traces of PCBs, but it was not possible to quantify their concentrations. Although only a few samples were analysed, the results show the presence of hazardous substances in the ecosystem. Further investigations of the presence of these and other substances in fish and agricultural products are necessary.

In some areas along the southern third of the coastline, demolition debris has been dumped on the beach and sand dunes. However, such dump sites are far more common and extensive further north, where significant portions of the houses and the coastal road have been at least partially built on dumped waste materials. With increasing coastal erosion obvious in areas such as Tel Katifa, west of El Nuseirat, Deir el Balah, Nezarim and several places further north, the waste will become exposed and cause additional pollution.

The observation of fishing activities along the coast shed some light on the state of fisheries in the Gaza

Table 18. Levels of pesticides and PCBs in biota (µg/kg of fat)

Pollutant	Mussels	Lizardfish (Aulopiformes)	Red mullet (Mullidae)	Juvenile snappers (Lutjanidae)	Grouper (Epinephelidae)
p,p-DDE	77	60	13	485	6
p,p-DDD	n.d.	n.d.	n.d.	28	n.d.
p,p-DDT	n.d.	n.d.	n.d.	27	n.d.
o,p-DDT	n.d.	n.d.	n.d.	47	n.d.
PCB	trace	trace	trace	trace	trace

n.d. = not detected

Buying fish at Gaza City market. Due to the security situation it was not possible to acquire the samples at sea

Environmental Assessment of the Gaza Strip

Table 19.   Analysis of sewage sludge on Gaza beach (21-SOIL-01) and Gaza City harbour sediment (32-SOIL-01) samples

Parameter	21-SOIL-01 (mg/kg)	LAGA List (mg/kg)	GSSO (mg/kg)	32-SOIL-01 (mg/kg)	Dutch List (mg/kg)
	Sewage sludge[a]	Z value	Limit value	Harbour sand	Intervention values
Pb	26	Z0 (<40)	900	22.5	530
Cd	<0.8	Z1 (<3)	10	<0.8	12
Cr	23.4	Z1 (<180)	900	11.2	380
Co	<10.0	N/A	N/A	<10.0	240
Cu	40.8	Z1 (<120)	800	24.6	190
Ni	<10.0	Z0 (<15)	200	15.6	210
Hg	0.33	Z1 (<1.5)	8	<0.01	10
Zn	296	Z1 (<450)	2,500	46.1	720

[a] According to EWC: 19 08 Wastes from wastewater treatment plants not otherwise specified, 19 08 05 sludge from treatment of urban wastewater.

One of many outfalls of untreated sewage into the Mediterranean Sea

Strip. Inspections of catches of fish in several places along the coast made clear that fishing is intensive and exceeds the optimal yield for most species. The catches are largely comprised of juvenile individuals that have not yet had a chance to reproduce. More detailed analysis of catches and catch statistics would be necessary to allow more precise conclusions about the status of the more important fish stocks in the Gaza coastal waters.

Soil samples from Gaza beach (21-SOIL-01) and Gaza harbour (32-SOIL-01) were collected to evaluate the impact on beach and harbour sediments (see Table 19).

At Gaza beach, the dried sewage sludge formed a crust on the beach sand that was apparently deposited at times of high water levels. Heavy metal contents qualify it as a Z1 waste, which should be deposited on a landfill site.

The Gaza harbour sediment has comparatively low contamination. Only nickel exceeds the LAGA Z0 value for waste, and none of the parameters reaches the Dutch List intervention values. The LAGA values are mentioned here, as the harbour is heavily sedimented. In case of dredging, sediment contamination must be taken into account to determine its future use. The sediment collected from the harbour was relatively coarse sand. Therefore, it can be assumed that heavy metal and other parameters are elevated in silt and mud, as contaminants tend to be absorbed to organic matter and clay minerals in the sediments.

3.4   Institutional assessment

Three key Palestinian institutions deal with environmental issues in the Gaza Strip. The first is the Environmental Quality Authority (EQA), which has overall oversight and regulatory authority on environmental matters. The EQA was established in 2002 as a successor to the Ministry of Environmental Affairs. It has two principal functions: (i) coordination between Palestinian environment-related governmental institutions, municipalities, non-governmental organizations (NGOs) and the private sector; and (ii) coordination between Palestinians and donors supporting environmental activities in the Gaza Strip and the West Bank. The second is the Palestinian Water Authority (PWA), which supervises and regulates issues related to water. Finally, there is the Coastal Municipalities Water Utility (CMWU), a government utility company formed by the 25 municipalities that use its services, and that is responsible for managing water and wastewater.

The proper functioning of these institutions has in varying degrees been hampered by the internal political situation that has prevailed in the Gaza Strip in recent years, and the escalation of hostilities in December 2008 and January 2009 further impacted their operations. While the EQA's building and assets (including environmental records) suffered direct physical damages, the mobility of staff from all institutions was restricted throughout the period, limiting their ability to effectively respond to urgent environmental problems that arose during the hostilities.

While key personnel in the PWA are still able to function, there is no oversight of well construction and water wells are being drilled in an uncontrolled manner, further damaging the aquifer. Also, as mentioned above, there is no adequate checking of the quality of water delivered by private companies, on which much of the population depends.

The CMWU has continued to function reasonably efficiently and to maintain the water supply systems and monitor water quality, but suffers from lack of funds and the restrictions on the import of goods into the Gaza Strip. These make the repair of the sewage system and water supply network a very challenging task.

Against this background, operational decisions about the environment are made by other government agencies, the private sector, the UN and NGOs. This can have environmental consequences as well. For example, the opening of the various dump sites discussed above has led to demolition rubble being dumped into the sea in an uncontrolled manner.

4   Recommendations

4.1   Introduction

The state of the environment in the Gaza Strip is bleak from any perspective. There are major challenges to be overcome across a broad range of environmental sectors, but particularly in relation to the over-use and contamination of groundwater. In addition, the reconstruction of damaged buildings and infrastructure will have its own environmental impacts.

Technical solutions are available, but implementing them requires financial resources, materials, equipment and technical expertise that are currently not available in the Gaza Strip. These environmental issues, however, will not be resolved on their own, and will only grow more serious with further delay. The specific technical recommendations proposed here are based on the assumption that the necessary financial and other resources will be found, and that the security situation will allow work to proceed on the ground.

Two sets of recommendations follow, based on the findings of the environmental assessment described in the previous chapter. The first are recommendations for the restoration of environmental damages that were directly caused by the escalation of violence in December 2008 and January 2009 (as detailed in Section 3.1). The second set of recommendations proposes measures to remediate pre-existing environmental degradation that was exacerbated by the recent events (as detailed in Section 3.2), which UNEP considers essential for improving the overall environmental situation in the Gaza Strip.

Workers recovering reinforcement bars from the rubble

4.2 Recommendations for the restoration of damage caused by the recent escalation of hostilities

Establish a facility to handle construction and demolition waste: Existing landfills do not have the space or the necessary controls to handle the large quantity of demolition rubble that was generated by the recent hostilities. A new facility, similar to the one created by UNDP to handle the demolition debris from the 2005 Gaza disengagement should be established. All efforts should be made to maximize recycling and reuse of the debris, including by crushing the rubble for reuse in the reconstruction work.

Systematically sort demolition rubble during the rubble removal phase: While the rubble itself may be non-hazardous, it is likely that there is contaminated material at all impacted sites. Care should be taken to identify such material, sort it onsite and dispose of it at a separate facility established for that purpose.

Perform due diligence. Every site that has been impacted during the recent events has the potential to have caused land contamination. This includes land below demolished buildings, locations were animal remains were buried, area impacted by spillage of sewage sludge, and craters on farmlands. Once these areas have been cleared of overlying materials, each of these locations needs to be assessed to ensure that there is no residual contamination posing long-term risk to the environment.

Provide technical support for farmland and orchard restoration: The destruction that was caused to farmland and orchards will need to be addressed if land degradation is to be mitigated in the long term. Efforts should be made to restore the vegetation cover as soon as possible to prevent desertification. At the same time, however, due to the change in the salinity of the irrigation water it may no longer be feasible to replant the same crops. Technical assistance should be given to the farmers to ensure that appropriate crops and irrigation systems are used.

Repair water supply and sewage systems: The water supply and sewage systems that were impacted by the hostilities, including water wells, need to be repaired. Some of these repairs have already been executed and the remainder need to be undertaken as a matter of priority, as damaged water supply and sewage systems often lead to water contamination and health impacts.

Dispose of hazardous materials in a controlled manner: The escalation of violence has resulted in the production of materials that cannot be handled in the same way as normal domestic waste. These include asbestos, oil-contaminated soil, chemically contaminated soil, sludge from sewage treatment plants and healthcare waste. A hazardous waste management facility should be identified in the region to handle this waste stream, or the waste sorting and due diligence efforts will be ineffective.

Ensure health and safety during demolition: Many buildings were partially damaged in the conflict, and demolition of these buildings is likely to lead to many health and safety challenges. The assistance of health and safety professionals specialized in building demolition will be required to ensure the safe demolition of large buildings.

4.3 Recommendations for the remediation of pre-existing environmental degradation that was exacerbated by the recent hostilities

Remove water from the ongoing conflict in the region: All parties to the conflict should be alerted to the challenges posed by the general environmental degradation in the Gaza Strip and efforts should be made at the highest possible political level to remove water resources from the conflict framework.

Provide safe water to infants: All evidence suggests that children in the Gaza Strip are currently at risk of consuming water with elevated levels of nitrates, which can lead to methemoglobinaemia, or "Blue Baby Syndrome". Immediate action should be taken to provide all children under one year old with clean and safe water.

Carry out a study on the prevalence of methemoglobinaemia: Due to the reported prevalence of methemoglobinaemia in the Gaza Strip, a comprehensive study should be undertaken. UN organizations including WHO, UNEP, UNICEF and UNRWA can provide technical support for such a study.

Rest the coastal aquifer: The aquifer is severely damaged and collapsing quickly. Unless the trend is reversed now, damage could take centuries to reverse. Since the aquifer is a continuum with Egypt and Israel, any such action must be coordinated with these countries. Ideally, abstraction from the aquifer should cease and a monitoring system should be installed to evaluate recovery. Controlled abstraction should only be permitted once the aquifer recovers and the sustainable yield is recalculated using accurate data on inflows.

Develop alternative water supply to the Gaza Strip: Alternative sources of water should be developed and used to allow the coastal aquifer to rest. The only method that can produce water in adequate quantities is seawater desalination. However, the salt and brine that are generated as side products constitute waste that may put the environment under additional stress if they are not handled appropriately.

Improve efficiency of the water supply network: Currently, only 57 percent of the water pumped into the network is accounted for, due mainly to leakages. The entire network should be repaired.

Eliminate all inflow of salty and nitrate-containing recharge into the groundwater: All entry of contaminated water into the coastal aquifer must be controlled. This includes sewage, agricultural run-off, and storm water run-off.

Dispose of all sewage deep offshore: All sewage that is currently pooled in the various lagoons should be drained into the sea. Until new and efficient sewage treatment plants are established, all sewage should be disposed at a safe distance and depth offshore, as an interim arrangement.

Establish new sewage treatment plant(s): One or more new modern sewage treatment plants should be constructed, which include the final step of denitrification so that the effluent can be reused for agricultural purposes. The sewage treatment plants should also comprise sewage sludge treatment facilities to compost, aerate or otherwise treat the sludge to enable its use in agriculture (only if heavy metals and other contaminants are present in low concentrations).

Improve the sewage system: Currently, only 64 percent of the population is connected to the sewage network and the remaining 36 percent disposes of sewage locally. This is causing nitrate pollution and salt accumulation in the coastal aquifer. As part of the aquifer rescue programme, the coverage of the sewage network should be extended to 100 percent of the population and the existing system refurbished.

Decontaminate sewage ponds and Wadi Gaza: Years of holding sewage (or draining as in the case of Wadi Gaza) have contaminated these locations with salt, nutrients and heavy metals. They need to be comprehensively assessed, the contaminated material removed and the locations restored. In the case of Wadi Gaza, its potential to be turned into a wetland again requires additional study.

Establish a modern solid waste management centre: The Gaza Strip will need at least one modern solid waste management centre for both domestic and hazardous wastes. It may be best to convert one of the existing locations into a site for a new landfill, but the landfill itself must be entirely new.

Establish a solid waste management system: The solid waste management centre is just one part of a waste management system. The system should provision for household separation, collection from households, transfer and transport, storage, treatment and final disposal of the waste.

Decommission existing landfills: All existing landfill sites, except the UNDP storage facility, need to be decommissioned. The sites should then be cleaned up and returned to alternative land uses after due environmental diligence.

Improve coastal protection: The dumping of demolition debris and garbage in the coastal area, the construction of houses and other infrastructure in the dunes, and the mining of sand should be managed so as to avoid serious degradation of the sensitive coastal ecosystem.

Rebuild environmental governance: Environmental sustainability depends on the ability of local authorities to monitor and manage their own environment. Environmental governance in the Gaza Strip has been weakened by internal political developments, as well as by the recent escalation of hostilities. A number of institutions will need to be supported in terms of technical assistance and operating funds. The EQA in particular needs to be rebuilt and properly staffed to enable it to play its central role in the environmental management of the Gaza Strip.

5 Economic assessment

5.1 Introduction

Economic evaluation of environmental damage is a reasonably well developed branch of applied economics. By the early 1990s, it was accepted by economists and decision-makers that the methods used were robust enough to serve as a basis for policy-making.[12] In addition, since the Exxon Valdez oil spill litigation in the early 1990s, environmental economics-based evaluations of environmental damages have been used to settle claims in legal disputes.[13] The technique is now routinely employed to value ecosystem services, tourist locations and air quality.

The usual components in such studies[14] are:

- cost of mitigation/replacement;

- assessment of damage through stated willingness to pay (avoid damage) or willingness to accept compensation;

- assessment of damage through revealed willingness to pay as evident from the cost of alternatives or the mitigating expenditure incurred by the people; and

- estimates developed elsewhere in similar contexts.[15]

However, the economic valuation of conflict-related environmental damage is fraught with methodological difficulties. Consequently, there are few examples of post-conflict economic assessments of environmental impacts. The first such study was the assessment of the countries impacted by the first Gulf War that was requested by the United Nations Compensation Commission, and on the basis of which Kuwait, Saudi Arabia, Jordan, Iran, Syria and Turkey submitted claims that have since been settled.

A second more recent example is the *"Economic assessment of environmental degradation due to July 2006 hostilities in the Republic of Lebanon"* that was carried out by the World Bank.[16] This study attempted to estimate the impact of the hostilities on the environment, and provided an "order of magnitude" estimate for the cost of environmental degradation. It calculated the value of the overall cost of the current and future impacts of the hostilities, with 2006 as the base year. This study, which was according to its authors the first published attempt to evaluate the cost of conflict-related environmental damage, shows that environmental assessments of this kind are inherently difficult due to the lack of available data.

In its Decision 25/12 on the environmental situation in the Gaza Strip, the Governing Council requested UNEP to carry out an economic evaluation of the rehabilitation and restoration of the environmental damage resulting from the escalation of hostilities in the Gaza Strip in December 2008 and January 2009. It is important to highlight that the economic evaluation that was requested was not an evaluation of the damage caused, but rather *an evaluation of the cost of rehabilitation and restoration*. This gave the exercise a broader scope, and made it forward-looking and practical.

5.2 Scope of the economic assessment

Based on the mandate from the Governing Council and input from the UNEP expert who visited the Gaza Strip in January 2009, terms of reference were prepared, which comprised the following key elements:

- cost of re-establishing the environmental and public health infrastructure damaged as a result of the recent hostilities;

- additional cost of handling, transporting and disposing of the solid wastes generated during the hostilities, minus any revenue generated from recycling construction materials;

- cost of clean-up and remediation of the contaminated land, plus the opportunity cost of taking land out of profitable use in the interim;

- cost of re-establishing environmental monitoring and information management systems that collapsed due to the recent hostilities and the ongoing blockade of goods and materials entering the Gaza Strip; and

- economic valuation of any recreational areas (such as beaches) that may have been impacted due to the conflict by the release of untreated sewage, solid wastes or hazardous materials.

The main environmental issues considered in the assessment were:

- demolition debris, which contain both non-hazardous and hazardous substances;
- damage to water and wastewater infrastructure;
- impact on solid waste management infrastructure; and
- land degradation.

5.3 Economic assessment methodology

It was explained in earlier sections of this report that while a number of environmental sectors were impacted by the escalation of hostilities in December 2008 and January 2009, not all environmental damage observed by UNEP in the Gaza Strip was directly caused by those events. It was therefore important that this distinction also be made when evaluating the cost of the environmental damage resulting from the recent hostilities. Of the four categories of environmental issues identified by the UNEP team (see Chapter 2), the economic assessment – like the environmental assessment – only considered the first two:

a) Environmental impacts that were visible and measurable at the time of the assessment, and could be demonstrated to be directly linked to the recent escalation of hostilities. This included issues such as the vast quantities of demolition rubble, the destruction of orchards, and damage to water supply and sewage networks: and

b) Environmental degradation that could be scientifically demonstrated to have been exacerbated by the hostilities, although the observed damage could not be entirely imputed to the recent events. This included issues such as groundwater pollution, sewage contamination and impacts on landfills.

It was also explained earlier that in analysing the environmental issues in the second category, it was not always scientifically possible to distinguish between pre-existing degradation and damage caused by the escalation of hostilities in December 2008-January 2009. Even so, it would not make sense to attempt to restore the environment to its pre-December 2008 state, as that state was unacceptable by international standards. The economic assessment, therefore, did not attempt to evaluate what fraction of the estimated restoration costs should be considered as a cost of the recent escalation of hostilities.

UNEP concluded that whenever a specific environmental damage could be clearly identified as having been caused by the recent hostilities, it would be analysed and quantified as an environmental cost of the recent events. With regard to restoration costs, however, UNEP recommended and costed full restoration of the environmental sector to internationally acceptable levels, without any consideration of the timeframe in which the environmental damage occurred. It is important that these estimates of the cost of restoration not be understood as the cost of the environmental damage caused by the recent hostilities, as in many cases only a fraction of the damage actually occurred during this period.

It was also necessary to define what constituted an environmental damage. If a particular building was damaged or destroyed during a conflict, the losses to its owner, to the people who live there and to those who are injured or killed were accounted for as direct losses, and excluded from an economic evaluation of environmental damages. Only the cost of handling the rubble in an environmentally responsible way was calculated, along with the cost of environmental due diligence work at the building site once the debris was cleared. When the structure impacted was part of the environmental infrastructure to begin with (water wells or sewage treatment plants) however, the cost of replacement or repair was included in the environmental costing.

In consideration of the above, the methodology used for the economic assessment was the following:

1. The first necessary step was the assessment of the environmental damages that were caused or exacerbated by the escalation of hostilities in December 2008 and January 2009. This survey was carried out by the UNEP expert team in May 2009 and is presented in earlier sections of this report. In cases where the damage had already been repaired (e.g. water distribution network) at the time of the field visit, reports

from the UNEP mission in January 2009 and from other UN agencies on the ground were used as records of the damage.

2. The Early Recovery Plan and detailed sectoral assessments conducted by various UN agencies in the Gaza Strip in the aftermath of the escalation of hostilities (see Appendix II) included estimates of the financial costs related to rebuilding or mitigating some of the damages caused by these events. These estimates were used as the starting point for evaluating environmental costs, but were refined by the information provided by the technical experts who carried out the field work.

3. The formula used for assessing economic cost was as follows: economic cost of mitigating environmental damage = (A) economic cost of the environmental loss + (B) economic cost of repairing/renovating the system, or of safe disposal. For example, the total cost of damages to the water supply network includes the losses suffered by the population until the network is rebuilt (A), as well as the cost of rebuilding it (B). The cost of rebuilding is provided by the Early Recovery Plan, and the cost of the impacts on the population before it is rebuilt can be estimated through the hypothetical cost of providing emergency water supply to the households until the network is repaired.

4. The financial costs of mitigating environmental damages were also analysed to determine whether they corresponded to economic costs. Economic costs consider the opportunity costs of inputs and outputs, rather than paid out costs. Wherever possible, attempts were made to convert financial costs into economic costs. If such a conversion was not possible due to lack of data, it was noted.

5. In addition, the difference between gross versus net losses, which is a significant issue when damage assessments are based on revenue loss in certain activities, had to be considered. The difference between net and gross loss can be illustrated by the following example: if tourism declines on a beach, there will be a loss of revenue. However the inputs (services, equipment, etc.) used to service tourists may be used elsewhere. Thus the loss, if estimated solely as the reduction in tourism revenue on a given beach, i.e. the gross loss, will be overestimated. Economists try to assess the net losses wherever possible by accounting for the existence of opportunities, if any, to use the inputs that become available due to the reduction of economic activities caused by the conflict elsewhere in the economy. For example, given the fact that there is a high level of unemployment in the Gaza Strip, environmental rehabilitation projects are likely to create more employment. This can be accounted for in economic cost accounting through shadow prices of labour.

6. Based on steps 1-5, the total economic costs of identified environmental damages resulting from the recent hostilities were estimated.

7. The final step was an order of magnitude costing of selected pre-existing critical environmental issues in the Gaza Strip, such as the over-abstraction of groundwater. This included the identification of possible solutions, and an estimate of the resources required to adequately address these issues. The costs of addressing these long-term environmental issues were based on an order of magnitude, as detailed engineering estimates were not available,

5.4 Limitations and constraints

Undertaking an economic assessment usually presupposes the existence of a market mechanism whereby input and output costs are determined by the market. In the Gaza Strip, however, the normal functioning of markets for goods, services, labour, capital and other inputs has been disrupted by ongoing conflict, and impaired by the restrictions on the movement of goods, materials and equipment to and from the area. The recent escalation of hostilities further aggravated the economic situation of the population. In the Gaza Strip, even people with productive assets do not earn an appropriate income.

This has implications for an environmental economic assessment, which places an emphasis on people's choices with regard to environmental services – choices usually assessed through their preference for goods and services, or through questionnaire surveys (as in the method of contingent valuation). Willingness to pay for environmental services is likely to be affected by income levels. Thus, the low income levels due to conflict lead to a low value for environmental goods and services. If people's economic activity is already severely limited, the economic loss associated with additional environmental impacts may become smaller and smaller.

This problem arises even when a "cost of mitigation" approach (rather than a "willingness-to-pay" approach) is used to value the environmental damage. For example, the cost of rubble removal is likely to be lower if more people are unemployed due to the conflict, so that the same environmental impact may result in lesser economic cost if the economy becomes increasingly dysfunctional as a result of conflict. By this token, the same physical damage in Beirut and in the Gaza Strip, for example, would translate into different environmental costs, the Gaza Strip being lower.

One solution is to use the cost of resources (including labour) on the basis of what prevails not in the society under evaluation, but in another society that has similar economic features but is not affected by conflict. The prospects for an assessment of this kind in the Gaza Strip were limited by the fact that engineering estimates of the cost of restoration in the recovery plan had already taken current local costs into account.

The design of this assessment and conditions in the Gaza Strip were such that long-term field studies or primary surveys could not be used. It was not possible to conduct primary data gathering on the damages suffered by the local population, or information about their perceptions or willingness to pay for restoration. Moreover, in many cases it was impossible to distinguish between current conditions and those that prevailed prior to the recent escalation of violence. The mitigation measures used in this assessment, for example in the case of the removal and disposal of construction debris, are likely to mitigate not only environmental losses, but also some direct losses.

Finally, in addition to those associated with the damage caused by the recent escalation of hostilities, the recovery effort itself will have environmental costs. For example the rebuilding of thousands of homes will require materials whose production and transportation will have an environmental footprint. While this footprint no doubt has an economic value, UNEP did not attempt to cost it as the environmental assessment did not include detailed life cycle analyses of the reconstruction process.

5.5   Findings

Environmental costs directly linked to the escalation of violence in December 2008 and January 2009

Rubble and asbestos

It is estimated that approximately 600,000 tonnes of rubble were generated by the collapse of buildings and other infrastructure during the escalation of violence. The quantity of rubble generated in various parts of the Gaza Strip is presented in Table 20. Plans are currently being developed for its removal, so that reconstruction efforts can begin.

Most of the buildings were not fully demolished, however, and still contain potentially hazardous materials. The presence of asbestos was observed in a number of locations, and other hazardous materials cannot be ruled out. These require safe handling since mixing the two waste streams would turn what is mostly non-hazardous demolition debris into hazardous waste. In addition, the removal of rubble from buildings that are not fully demolished poses a health and safety threat to those working at the site as well to neighbours, and hence adequate care and safeguards need to be taken.

Table 20.   Quantity of construction debris in the Gaza Strip (Source: UNDP/PAPP May 2009)

Area	Estimated quantity of rubble (tonnes)
Gaza City	216,571
North Area	158,606
Middle Area	58,850
Khan Yunis	54,068
Rafah	100,541
Total	**588,637**

The assessment methodology considers two costs: (A) the cost of the damage until repair/disposal; and (B) the final cost of repair/disposal. In this case, the calculation of A is difficult due to lack of data on any specific environmental damage caused by the rubble or other materials contained within. Thus, the economic cost in this case takes into account only B – the final cost of removal.

The report *Public services and roads in the Gaza Strip after the last 22 days of war in Gaza,* prepared by UNDP,[17] provides information about the quantity of rubble and the financial cost of removing it. The financial cost is estimated as USD 10 per tonne for sorting and transportation to the dump site. Thus, the cost of removal and disposal of the rubble is estimated to be approximately USD 6 million.

This estimate does not take into account the asbestos content in the rubble and possible presence of other hazardous materials, and the safeguards required for its safe disposal. UNEP estimates that an increase of approximately 20 percent in the per-unit cost is needed to sort and dispose of rubble since it is necessary to take into account the safe handling that is dictated by the presence of asbestos. Thus, the cost of safe removal and transportation of the total volume of rubble is calculated at USD 7.2 million.

Since the buildings in the Gaza Strip were destroyed or damaged during conflict, it is necessary to carry out systematic environmental due diligence at affected sites before returning the land to its original use or assigning it a new use. It is estimated that the cost of environmental due diligence, per site, will average USD 1,500. Given that there are 2,692 affected sites, the total cost of environmental due diligence would be USD 4,038,000.

Currently, there is no facility within the Gaza Strip for recycling rubble, so a disposal site is required. A safe disposal location also needs to be found for the other hazardous materials found within the rubble. Wherever these disposal facilities are identified, they should be located away from the community to prevent health risks to people from the hazardous chemicals and the noise and particulate damage from the handling of rubble. The current landfills in the Gaza Strip do not have sufficient space to accommodate this rubble or facilities for hazardous materials. Therefore,

Box 3.   Calculation of land needed for the safe dumping of rubble

Quantity of rubble: 600,000 tonnes

Volume of rubble: 500,000 cubic metres (with an assumption of bulk density of 1.2 tonnes/m^3)

Area required if the height of dumping is limited to 5 metres: 100,000 square metres

Safe area around dumping ground: 25 percent of the dumping site

Total area required: 125,000 square metres (125 dunums)

Social cost of land: USD 6,250,000 (with a cost assumption of USD 50,000 per dunum)

Table 21.   Costs of the removal and safe disposal of rubble and asbestos

Item	Costs (USD million)
Direct cost for removal and transportation	6.00
Cost of safeguards due to the presence of asbestos fibre	1.20
Environmental due diligence cost	4.04
Social cost of land to be used as disposal site	6.25
Total	**17.49**

new land will have to be made available for this purpose, which comes with a social cost, even if public land is used. The area of land required and the calculated cost are shown in Box 3.

Thus, the total cost for the removal of rubble containing asbestos is USD 17,488,000. A breakdown is provided in Table 21.

The estimated quantity of rubble may also include some useful components, such as steel, which could be recovered at the time of removal. Though, strictly speaking, this needs to be accounted for, it can be excluded due to the relative small proportion of such materials in the overall waste, as well as the cost of extraction of such materials.

Handling of solid and hazardous waste

After the recent escalation of hostilities, all municipalities in the Gaza Strip reported that solid waste had accumulated in the streets. Some landfill

Environmental Assessment of the Gaza Strip

sites could not be accessed due to ongoing fighting, and this forced municipalities to keep solid waste in temporary locations, including a site that was already full. Some 20,000 tonnes of solid waste accumulated in the Rafah area. The financial cost of expanding and rehabilitating existing landfills was estimated at USD 4 million, while the expected expenditure of restoring solid waste containers was valued at USD 0.108 million. Damage to trucks used for solid waste disposal was valued at USD 0.685 million.

In addition, lack of adequate power supply during the conflict prevented many hospitals and healthcare centres from properly disposing of medical waste. This led to HHCW being mixed with domestic waste. Assessing this cost was a challenge

as the mixed waste had already been dumped in the landfills and would not cause immediate damage. The costs associated with solid waste management (excluding rubble and asbestos) are summarized in Table 22.

Table 22. Cost of restoring the solid waste management system (excluding rubble and asbestos)

Item	Cost (USD million)
Cost of expanding and rehabilitating landfills	4.000
Restoring solid waste containers	0.108
Repairing damage to trucks for solid waste transportation	0.685
Total	**4.793**

In the absence of effective public systems, private waste collectors have entered the market

Damages to the water and sanitation network

Before the recent hostilities, the Gaza Strip had 97 percent water supply coverage at 80 litres per capita per day, and 64 percent sewage collection and treatment coverage. The water supply was often saline, however, and was well below international standards of drinking. Recent hostilities are reported to have damaged 11 wells and four reservoirs, as well as 19,920 metres of water pipes and 2,445 metres of sewage pipe network. Damages occurred in four locations of the sewage network and pumping stations, the North Gaza sewage treatment plant, water utility premises and many household water storage systems.[18] The damage to the electricity network and the power shortages also affected the normal water supply and wastewater pumping and treatment in the Gaza Strip.

As a result, it is reported that nearly 840 households (with an average family size of around 7.25 persons) suffered damage to their water supply. A further 5,200 households lost their roof water tanks, and another 2,355 tanks suffered damage. The *Gaza Situation Report*[19] states that nearly 10 percent of the population of the Gaza Strip did not receive proper water supplies immediately after the cessation of hostilities, and a population of 32,000 did not have access to proper water supply even three months after the ceasefire was concluded. Other households may also have been indirectly affected.

A number of environmental and health impacts may be related to these damages:

- lack of good quality water may lead to an increase in disease;

- water and sewage water may mix, exacerbating health problems;

- sewage from damaged treatment plants may be released onto agricultural and other land; and

- untreated or undertreated sewage may be drained out to sea, causing problems to the marine environment, and for people using the sea.

The costs of the damage are summarized in Table 23.

Health-related damages

Though epidemiological patterns are monitored weekly in the Gaza Strip, the reports do not show any clear trend for most diseases during the period immediately following the recent hostilities. Monitoring was less than satisfactory during the hostilities themselves, but became fully functional again afterwards. In the case of watery diarrhoea, the data shows that there was a 13 percent increase during six weeks in January and February, as compared to the corresponding period of 2008, although no increase was recorded between levels reported immediately before and after the crisis.[20] A higher incidence of this disease was also reported among children who attended UNRWA clinics from areas affected by water contamination, while it was not reported among children from areas where there was no water contamination. The public health laboratory noted that 12-14 percent of the water

Table 23.   Environmental costs associated with the damages to the water supply and wastewater collection and treatment

Damages until final mitigation (A)	Assessing economic costs	Cost of mitigation (B)	Assessing economic costs
Lack of quality water immediately after the disruption creating health problems	Assess either the costs due to increased disease prevalence, or assess the cost of providing emergency supply of similar amount of water – the latter is attempted since data are not available for the former	Restore water networks and home connections	Financial cost
Spillage of sewage into agri-cultural land	Direct cost of decontaminating land flooded with sewage water; Opportunity cost of leaving land fallow for a year (with the assumption that after one year, such land can be cultivated again)		Financial cost
Drainage of sewage into sea	Lack of adequate data to differentiate recent impacts	Restore sewage treatment plants	Financial cost

Box 4.   Calculation of the hypothetical cost of providing emergency water supply to people affected by the damage to the water and wastewater network

Number of people without quality water supply for one month
= 150,000 (10 percent of the population)

Number of people likely to be affected until the full restoration is made
= 40,000

Time needed for full restoration = 200 days

Quantum of drinking water supply per day = 150,000 * 2 litres per capita per day for 30 days
+ 40,000 * 2 litres per capita per day for 200 days = 25,000,000 litres

Quantum of domestic water supply per day = 150,000 * 100 litres per capita per day for 30 days
+ 40,000 * 100 litres per capita per day for 200 days = 1,250,000,000 litres

Cost of providing emergency drinking water supply = 25,000,000 * USD 0.02 per litre
= USD 500,000

Cost of providing emergency domestic water supply = 1,250,000,000 * USD 0.002 per litre
= USD 2,500,000

Total cost of emergency water supply to compensate for the damage = USD 3 million

samples collected immediately after the hostilities contained total coliform and faecal coliform.[21] This level of contamination, according to the report, is 50 percent higher than the average level of contamination detected prior to the crisis.

However, these indications of health issues may be only a part of the costs borne by the population due to the water pollution caused by damage to water and wastewater networks. In addition, the fact that no increase in the incidence of other diseases was reported does not rule them out. Some problems may not become serious or may take time to manifest themselves. The absence of disease, despite water pollution, may be the result of increased caution and care by individuals or medical systems – which may involve additional costs. Thus, any attempt to cost the increased incidence of some diseases[22] will underestimate the total costs attributed to water pollution and shortages due to recent hostilities.

Instead of valuing all such losses, this assessment used a cost of mitigation approach to estimate health and other damages due to water pollution and shortages. This was calculated by estimating the cost of a hypothetical emergency water supply to the affected population until such time as a fully fledged piped water supply system could be

made functional and wastewater networks could be repaired to avoid any contamination of the water supply. This calculation is shown in Box 4. The total cost is estimated as USD 3 million.

Damage to Az Zaitoun wastewater treatment plant

The damage to the Gaza Strip's sewage treatment plant is reported to have caused a spillage of 100,000 cubic metres of sewage inundating approximately 55,000 square metres (55 dunums) of land. The UN Early Recovery Plan included an estimate of USD 0.33 million to decontaminate land flooded with wastewater. In addition, this land will be unsuitable for cultivation for a period of one to two years, depending on when the detailed assessment can be completed. The damage on this count is the lost agricultural income from this area. UNEP does not have clear estimates of agricultural income from this land, thus an indirect estimate was used. Given that the current price of one dunum of land (1,000 square metres) is likely to be between USD 10,000 and 100,000 (with a median value of around USD 50,000), the value of net income from land is taken to be USD 5,000 per dunum per year. This net income can be interpreted as the net value addition, i.e. the returns to the land owner plus labour, or the gross income minus the

Table 24. Components of the direct costs of restoring water supply and waste-water collection and treatment

Item	Cost (USD million)
Restore water networks and home connections	4.84
Reconstruct and restore water wells, reservoirs and wastewater collection networks	1.02
Restore basins and inlet pressure pipelines for Gaza emergency sewage treatment plant	0.18
Reconstruct wastewater facilities	0.13
Total	**6.17**

non-labour cost of cultivation. The gain for labour can also be included due to the lack of adequate employment opportunities there. Thus, the cost of taking 50 dunums out of cultivation for one year is estimated at USD 275,000 (55 * 5000).

Restoring the water and wastewater infrastructure

The other element of the environmental cost is that of restoring and repairing the damaged water and wastewater network and treatment plants. The financial costs associated with these initiatives are listed in Table 24.

How these financial costs reflect economic costs depends on whether or not the financial expenditure on different inputs reflects their opportunity costs. As mentioned in the case of rubble removal, the budgeted expenditure for wages may be higher than the current opportunity costs of labour due to the high levels of unemployment in Gaza, but lower than the potential wage rate in the region for non-conflict contexts. There is therefore no adjustment for labour cost. Moreover, a major part of the cost of rebuilding the water and wastewater network is capital cost, for which there is no reason for the financial costs to diverge significantly from the economic costs. Given this situation and the lack of reliable information, the economic cost here is understood to be the same as the financial cost (USD 6.17 million).

Damage due to the release of sewage into the sea

The damage to wastewater treatment plants has led to the release of untreated and undertreated sewage into the sea. This has polluted the marine

environment, with implications for marine biodiversity, fisheries and the health of communities using the sea for recreational activities. However, assessing this aspect of economic loss is a major challenge, since incompletely treated sewage was regularly discharged into the sea before the recent escalation of hostilities and it is therefore not possible to measure the additional pollution caused by recent events.

As mentioned in Chapter 3, children and families continue to swim and play in polluted waters. However, reliable data on the extent of the pollution preceding the recent hostilities, as well as the number of families regularly using the sea and any manifested health impacts is not available. Even if it were, assessing how pollution affects the marine environment and human health would require detailed scientific studies. It was thus not possible to make an informed assessment of this aspect of economic damage. Nevertheless, it should not be construed that the pollution of the seawater has no cost, or that Gaza's beaches have no economic value.

An alternate approach would have been to conduct a travel cost survey of beach users or a willingness-to-pay survey of communities along the coastline. Given that the Gaza Strip is not a fully functioning market, however, any such surveys would likely have resulted in gross underestimations of the economic value.

Damage to groundwater from sewage

The situation with respect the potential contamination of groundwater due to the damage to sewage treatment plants in the Gaza Strip is similar. There are two main issues to consider. First, given the absence of data, it is almost impossible to assess the additional damage caused by the recent hostilities. Second, as sewage treatment was not complete even before the recent hostilities, there could have been pre-existing contamination of groundwater by sewage. Therefore, no attempt was made to assess the impact of sewage on groundwater pollution. The pollution of groundwater by sewage and other sources constitutes a critical long-term environmental issue for the Gaza Strip, however, and the cost of rehabilitating the groundwater is discussed in the final section of this economic assessment.

The costs of the damages to water and wastewater networks are summarized in Table 25.

Table 25. Environmental costs due to damages to the water supply and wastewater collection and treatment systems

Item	Cost (USD million)
Hypothetical cost of emergency water supply to the affected people as a proxy to estimate the health damages due to lack of access to water supply immediately after the hostilities	3.00
Direct cost of decontaminating land flooded with wastewater	0.33
Opportunity cost of land flooded with wastewater being unavailable for cultivation up to two years	0.50
Total	**3.83**

Environmental damages due to crop loss and land contamination

The FAO has reported that the recent hostilities in the Gaza Strip led to the destruction of crops over 24,820,000 square metres (14.6 percent of 170,000,000) of land.[23] The damage to farmers was considered a direct loss and was hence not included in the calculation of environmental damages. However, as explosives impacted a number of these locations and some areas could still contain explosive remnants of war, farming has not resumed in every location across the Gaza Strip. There will, therefore, be the cost of environmental due diligence at these sites, as well as the opportunity cost of leaving the land fallow until due diligence is completed. According to UNOSAT estimates, 714 impact craters were observed on open ground and cultivated land in the Gaza Strip immediately after the ceasefire. The damaged cultivated area is estimated to be 2,100 hectares. Using the same method as for the area impacted by sewage (taking USD 50,000 as the average price of land per dunum, or 1,000 square metres, and taking one-tenth of this value as the annual net income from agriculture) the damage can be estimated as USD 10.5 million. There is also the cost of environmental due diligence to be conducted at each of the impact craters, which is calculated as an average of USD 1,500 per site, giving a total of USD 1,071,000.

As mentioned above, agricultural damage, including the loss of cultivated trees and plants, was considered to be a direct loss and was not included as an environmental cost. As the Gaza Strip is a highly cultivated area, with minimal space for natural growth, no loss of biodiversity is likely to have occurred. Moreover, there is no evidence to show that the varieties of trees cultivated on the damaged land were unique to the area or unavailable in other parts of the Gaza Strip or in the region. Thus, no attempt was made to account for the loss of biodiversity.

A loss in terms of carbon sequestration due to the destruction of trees may occur, though it is likely to be very small. Even in the best of biomass growing areas, annual growth is usually less than 8 tonnes per hectare (a carbon equivalent of around 4 tonnes per hectare). Such growth is unlikely in the climatic conditions of the Gaza Strip. Even if a carbon intake of 4 tonnes per hectare is assumed, the loss in one year due to the destruction of crops over 24,820,000 square metres (2,482 hectares) of land represents 9,928 tonnes of carbon intake. Assuming that currently 1 tonne of carbon emission leads to a loss of USD 15-20,[24] the total loss would be USD 148,920. This is likely to be an upper bound estimate, as crop growth in the Gaza Strip is not likely to be around 8 tonnes per hectare.

The environmental costs due to damages resulting from the recent escalation of hostilities and possible contamination of agricultural land are summarized in Table 26.

Nuisance costs

The damages arising from the hostilities are likely to create a number of nuisance-related issues for the population of the Gaza Strip. These include the stench emanating from broken sewage pipes, animal carcasses and solid waste strewn around the streets. People living near landfills and sewage treatment plants may experience additional nuisances due to overloading, incomplete treatment or even spillage of waste and sewage. Though there is no doubt that such nuisances have occurred, costing them is challenging in the absence of willingness-to-pay surveys. Since this study was concerned with the immediate

Table 26. Costs of damages and suspected contamination of agricultural land

Item	Cost (USD million)
Opportunity cost of land inaccessible for human use for a year due to suspected contamination, as a proxy of environmental damages	10.500
Cost of due diligence prior to allowing re-cultivation of land	1.071
Carbon sequestration losses due to the losses of trees and plants	0.148
Total	**11.719**

environmental impacts of to the recent hostilities (as opposed to nuisance issues related to longstanding environmental problems), it was not possible to use alternative methods such as hedonic pricing, based on land values in areas with higher levels nuisance. No costs were therefore calculated.

Another important reason why the assessment of nuisance cost is challenging is that environmental nuisance is routinely tolerated as part of everyday life in the Gaza Strip. Children playing in the sea contaminated by sewage is one such example. Indeed, years of economic deprivation, political instability and conflict have seemingly made the population of the Gaza Strip resigned to a lower quality of life.

Environmental footprint of recovery operations

In addition to the issues considered above, it is necessary to take into account the environmental footprint of the reconstruction operations that will have to be undertaken to restore the Gaza Strip at least to pre-December 2008 levels. Taking all the inputs required for the reconstruction of the Gaza Strip and assessing their ecological footprint is a complex undertaking and was not attempted for this study.

In order to understand the scale of the impact, one sector was considered: the reconstruction of damaged buildings. Expenditure on this item is about 25 percent of the total budget of rehabilitation cost. Given that other items in the recovery plan, such as the provision of social security benefits, are unlikely to make a significant impact in terms of ecological footprint, the impact of the reconstructing buildings is likely to take a larger share.

The recent hostilities destroyed 4,036 housing units. Ten schools, 14 mosques and a number of public buildings were also destroyed. New buildings totalling 665,693 square metres need to be built to replace residential buildings lost in the violence. If schools, mosques and other public buildings are replaced, this total could increase to 675,000 square metres. Accounts of the energy requirements for, and carbon emissions involved in, building construction are found in the literature.[25] These show that building construction (including the service connections) requires an average of around 5,600 megajoules per square metre, and emits carbon dioxide to the level of 460 kilogrammes per square metre. Following these rates, the reconstruction of damaged buildings in the Gaza Strip would require 3,780,000,000 megajoules of energy and would release 310,500 tonnes of carbon dioxide.

This is only a part of the environmental footprint, however. Another issue is the sourcing of construction materials, in particular sand, which will likely be extracted locally, further damaging sand dunes, degrading land and promoting desertification. No attempt has been made to cost this damage but these issues must be considered during reconstruction. Most other building materials (wood, steel, bricks, and stones) will need to be imported from outside the Gaza Strip, and will hence have an external environmental footprint.

Other damages

Several other environmental impacts are not valued separately in this assessment. For example, chemical contamination may arise from damage to industrial facilities and educational buildings, but additional safeguard measures taken during the removal of rubble are expected to address this issue. To some extent, this is also true of UXO. On the other hand, conflict-related materials remaining on agricultural land are considered part of land contamination, and taken into account accordingly.

There may also be some environmental issues related to damage to the electricity network. During or immediately after the recent hostilities, 35 percent of households in the Gaza Strip were without electricity. This figure had declined to 5 percent by 19 February. Fuel shortages also created problems, as the use of diesel and white diesel for cooking increased, leading to pollution. The substitution of cooking oil for regular fuel in cars, which occurs when gasoline or diesel are not available, also created environmental hazards. However, assessment of these damages was not attempted, due to the lack of any air quality data. It should also be noted that fuel shortages and related pollution have been a longstanding issue in the Gaza Strip, and therefore pre-date the recent hostilities.

Damage to the road network also falls in the category of excluded damages – 167 km of roads and two bridges were destroyed during the recent hostilities. This represents a direct loss to the road infrastructure, and must be repaired. In other contexts, damage to the road network would have increased traffic congestion and therefore pollution, which have a computable environmental cost. However given the low traffic density in the Gaza Strip – where donkey carts remain a key mode of transportation – road damages are unlikely to have led to large-scale environmental issues. While there are other factors influencing traffic movement in the Gaza Strip, including lack of adequate income-generating activities and the reliable supply of fuel, isolating the impact of recent events would have been a major challenge and was not attempted.

The people of the Gaza Strip have only very limited access to the sea due to military restrictions. Thus, most fishing boats operate within 2-3 kilometres of land. This may have led to over-fishing in the coastal area. However, the natural resource depletion due to over-fishing this limited area cannot be assessed due to lack of fisheries data. If such data had been available, over-fishing would have been reflected in the increase in the marginal cost of fishing.

Summary of environmental costs directly linked to the escalation of violence in December 2008 and January 2009

As demonstrated in the environmental assessment, the escalation of hostilities in December 2008 and January 2009 had significant environmental impacts. Some of these are clearly and directly attributable to the recent hostilities. Table 27 summarizes the environmental costs of these damages discussed in preceding sections.

Table 27. Environmental costs of damage directly linked to the escalation of hostilities in December 2008 and January 2009

Environmental damage	Associated cost (USD million)
Removal and safe disposal of rubble and asbestos	17.49
Restoring the solid waste management system	4.79
Direct cost of restoring water and wastewater systems	6.17
Environmental costs linked to water and wastewater systems	3.83
Cost associated with dealing with the damages and suspected contamination of agricultural land	11.72
Total	**44.00**

Costs of remediating long-term environmental issues in the Gaza Strip

In addition to the environmental impacts of the recent escalation of violence, the population of the Gaza Strip suffers from environmental pollution and natural resource depletion related to the ongoing political situation and associated problems, which limit human, social and economic development. As explained in the environmental assessment, some of these environmental issues were further exacerbated by the escalation of hostilities in December 2008 and January 2009.

One critical environmental issue is related to the serious water quality problems faced by the Gaza Strip.[26] Indeed, only 10 percent of the water sourced within the Gaza Strip is suitable for drinking. The main source of water is from wells dug in the coastal aquifer. Seventy percent of the water pumped out is used for irrigation. Though there is currently no water shortage in the Gaza Strip (except in Rafah Governorate), water will become scarcer in the future. Even at present, water distribution efficiency is only around 50-60 percent, a level that reflects the high number of leakages, unofficial connections to the water supply, and the amount of unmet demand. UNEP's assessment has demonstrated that no more wells can be dug in the Gaza Strip without exacerbating the salinity problem.

The Coastal Aquifer Management Plan (CAMP)[27] conducted a comprehensive evaluation of the status of the aquifer and proposed an overall plan for recovery that included the following recommendations:

- reduce abstraction of groundwater by increasing the supply of alternative sources of water, primarily desalinated water;

- improve treatment of sewage and use treated sewage for irrigation;

- reduce loss of water in the distribution network; and

- improve the sewage network to connect more of the population and reduce pollution of groundwater from cesspools.

In 2000, the overall cost of implementation of the CAMP was estimated at USD 1.7 billion over 20 years. Due to the political situation in the region, however, the CAMP has not been implemented. New estimates based on updated water requirements and sewage treatment needs are presented in Table 28. These figures should be taken as a preliminary order of magnitude estimate to demonstrate the scale of the problem rather than a full costing based on detailed engineering. Once there is consensus on the need for action and indications that resources are available, the appropriate engineering solutions can be developed, compared and costed.

From an economic assessment perspective, it should be noted that the severe water salinity issue in the Gaza Strip is an outcome of the longstanding political situation in the region. This is manifested not only in the lack (or slow implementation) of projects to provide alternative water sources, but also in the fact that many people in the Gaza Strip do not have alternative employment opportunities, forcing them to depend on water-inefficient agriculture.

Resolving the regional political conflict could improve the water situation in the Gaza Strip. It would open up the manufacturing and service sectors (including tourism), creating employment within the Gaza Strip and allowing its people to work elsewhere. This would reduce dependence on agriculture and thus water abstraction, permitting water use to become more compatible with the hydrological balance.

A second critical condition for the sustainable environmental development of the Gaza Strip is the restoration and rebuilding of environmental governance institutions. As discussed previously, the Palestinian EQA lost staff, equipment and data as a result of the recent hostilities, and no systematic environmental monitoring systems are currently in place. In order to restore and sustain the environment, both environmental institutions and environmental monitoring will need to be strengthened. The cost required for this has been calculated and is shown in Table 28.

Table 28.   Damages to environmental sectors, necessary actions and respective costs

	Damaged environmental sector	Action needed	Basis of costing	Order of magnitude estimates (in USD)
1	Damage to coastal aquifer			
		Develop alternative water sources	Cost of building and operating new desalination plant	400 million CAPEX (over 20 years) + 30 million OPEX per year for 20 years
2	Pollution of coastal aquifer			
		Decommission sewage ponds	Clean-up costs for the sewage ponds	10 million
		Clean and restore infiltration ponds	Clean-up costs	2 million
		Improve irrigation system to prevent agricultural leachate	Cost of high-efficiency irrigation systems	
		Establish new sewage treatment plants	Cost of new sewage treatment plant and its operation	265 million + 10 million per year for next 20 years
		Offshore disposal of sewage till sewage treatment plants fully functional	Cost of offshore pipelines	25 million
3	Land degradation			
		Decommissioning of landfills	Cost of decommissioning landfills	20 million
		Establishing new solid waste management facilities	Cost of new solid waste management centre	23 million + 2 million per year
4	Pollution of Wadi Gaza			
		Clean-up of Wadi Gaza sediments	Cost of rehabilitation of Wadi Gaza	5 million
5	Decline of environmental governance			
		Re-establishing EQA building and equipment	Cost or restoration	10 million
		Retraining for staff	Training costs	1 million
		Establish groundwater monitoring system	Cost of establishing and maintaining the groundwater monitoring system	5 million CAPEX + 1 million OPEX per year
		Establish marine monitoring system	Same for marine monitoring	1 million CAPEX + 500,000 OPEX

Endnotes

1. http://www.bmu.de/files/pdfs/allgemein/application/pdf/abfklaerv_aenderung_uk.pdf

2. http://www.reliefweb.int/rw/RWFiles2009.nsf/FilesByRWDocUnidFilename/PSLG-7QHJQZ-full_report.pdf/$File/full_report.pdf

3. 1 dunum = 1,000m²

4. Damage assessment report from the agriculture sector conducted by UNDP/PAPP

5. Coastal Municipalities Water Utility (CMWU). (2008). *Upgrading Gaza wastewater treatment plant.* http://www.iugaza.edu.ps/emp/emp_folders/99321/Upgrading_GWWTP.pdf

6. Emergency Water and Sanitation Hygiene (EWASH). (2009). *A brief outline of the sewage infrastructure and public health risks in the Gaza Strip for the World Health Organization.* http://www.ochaopt.org/cluster/admin/output/files/SewageInfrastructureGazaMarch2009WASHCluster-20090416-114157.pdf

7. Office for the Coordination of Humanitarian Affairs. (2009). *Emergency response to untreated sewage disposal into the Wadi Gaza, Gaza Strip.* https://www.ochaopt.org/caprevised/cap28.pdf

8. UNDP/PAPP. "Ambassador Chamberlin and UNDP visit Wadi Gaza Nature Park." Press release, 17 September 2003. http://www.papp.undp.org/en/newsroom/pressreleasespdf/2003/9a.pdf

9. Johansson, Nils. (2007). *Ecosystem management under stress conditions: The rise and fall of ecosystem management in a wetland landscape of the Central Gaza Strip.* http://stockholmresilience.org/download/18.aeea46911a31274279800082888/Johansson+NGG+07+Thesis.pdf

10. World Health Organization. (2009). *Gaza Strip initial health needs assessment.* http://www.ochaopt.org/gazacrisis/admin/output/files/ocha_opt_orgnizations_report_early_health_assessment_2009_02_16_english.pdf

11. World Health Organization. (2009). *Gaza Strip initial health needs assessment.* http://www.ochaopt.org/gazacrisis/admin/output/files/ocha_opt_who_gaza_situation_report_2009_02_04_english.pdf

12. A number of compendiums of case studies, evaluation techniques and training manuals are available. See Dixon and Hufschmidt, 1986; McCracken and Abaza, 2001; Bolt et al., 2005).

13. See NOAA Panel, 1993; Cohen, 1995; and Carson et al., 2004.

14. For instance, the *Economic assessment of environmental degradation due to July 2006 hostilities in the republic of Lebanon – A Sector Note*, carried out in 2007 by the World Bank (see World Bank 2007)

15. Ready R., S.Navrud (2006). "International benefit transfers: Methods and validity tests." *Ecological Economics*, 60:429-434.

16. World Bank. (2007). *Economic assessment of environmental degradation due to July 2006 hostilities in the Republic of Lebanon -- a Sector Note.*

17. UNDP/PAPP. (2009). *Public services and roads in Gaza Strip after the last 22 days of war on Gaza.* http://www.ochaopt.org/gazacrisis/infopool/opt_env_undp_Rubble_Circumstances_in_Gaza_Strip_feb_2009.pdf

18. United Nations Children's Fund (UNICEF). (2009). *Initial field assessment: Water, Sanitation and Hygiene*
    http://www.ochaopt.org/gazacrisis/infopool/opt_wash_cluster_Initial_Field_Assessment_jan_2009.pdf

19. WHO. (2009). *The Gaza Situation Report*.

20. See WHO. (2009). *Epidemiological Bulletins of Gaza*.

21. See WHO. (2009). *Epidemiological Bulletins of Gaza*.

22. There are attempts to calculate the economic losses of waterborne diseases outbreak, see Harrington et al. (1989), for example

23. FAO (2009). "Impact of Gaza crisis". *Agriculture Sector Report*. Palestine National Authority, Gaza.
    http://www.apis.ps/documents/AGR%20Sector%20Gaza%20Report_final.pdf

24. Based on a revision of the estimate given in Brown and Pearce 1994, as used in Santhakumar and Chakraborty 2003.

25. See Lee, K., Y. Choi, C. Chae, and B. Jung, (2007). *The Estimation of the Energy Consumption and CO_2 Emission at the Construction Stage*, Andong National University, Republic of Korea.

26. See Abu Nasar et al. 2007; All-Yaqubi et al. n.d.; Yaqubi 2008; Zakout 2007

27. Metcalf & Eddy AECOM, *Gaza Coastal Aquifer Management Program*.

Appendix I: UNEP Governing Council Decision 25/12: The environmental situation in the Gaza Strip

The Governing Council,

Recalling decision GCSS.VII/7 of 15 February 2002 on the environmental situation in the occupied Palestinian territories,

Recalling also the desk study on the environment in the occupied Palestinian territories published by the United Nations Environment Programme in 2003 and the environmental assessment of the areas disengaged by Israel in the Gaza Strip issued by the United Nations Environment Programme in 2006,

Noting with appreciation the participation of the United Nations Environment Programme in the United Nations-led early recovery rapid needs assessment mission carried out from 25 January to 4 February 2009,

Emphasizing the need for States to protect and preserve the environment in accordance with their international legal obligations,

Taking into account the 1992 Rio Declaration on Environment and Development[1] and all its relevant principles,

Expressing its deep concern at the negative implications of the environmental impacts on the Gaza Strip caused by the escalation of violence and hostilities during December 2008 and January 2009,

Noting with great concern the environment in the Gaza Strip,

1. *Requests* the United Nations Environment Programme to participate in the March 2009 Cairo conference on the reconstruction of Gaza, at which the report entitled "Gaza Early Recovery Rapid Needs Assessment" will be presented;

2. *Requests* the Executive Director of the United Nations Environment Programme to deploy immediately thereafter a mission of environmental experts to Gaza in coordination with other relevant international organizations to assess the natural and environmental impacts on the Gaza Strip caused by the escalation of violence and hostilities; to carry out an economic evaluation of the rehabilitation and restoration of the environmental damage; and to report to the Secretary-General thereon;

3. *Also requests* the Executive Director of the United Nations Environment Programme to initiate and facilitate the implementation of the recommendations made in the desk study on the environment in the occupied Palestinian territories published by the United Nations Environment Programme in 2003 and the environmental assessment of the areas disengaged by Israel in the Gaza Strip issued by the United Nations Environment Programme in 2006;

4. *Calls upon* the parties concerned to protect the environment as a matter of mutual interest in the region;

5. *Calls upon* member States and United Nations agencies to allocate adequate resources and provide technical, logistical and financial support and assistance to ensure the success of the United Nations Environment Programme mission of environmental experts to the Gaza Strip; and to implement the recommendations of the above-mentioned United Nations Environment Programme studies;

6. *Requests* the Executive Director of the United Nations Environment Programme to submit a follow-up report on the findings, results and recommendations to the Governing Council/Global Ministerial Environment Forum at its eleventh special session, in 2010

---

1) *Report of the United Nations Conference on Environment and Development*, Rio de Janeiro, 3-14 June 1992
(United Nations publication, Sales No. E.93.I.8 and corrigenda), vol. I: Resolutions adopted by the Conference, resolution 1, annex I.

Appendix II: List of assessments conducted in the Gaza Strip after the recent escalation of violence and hostilities

Medecins Du Monde – France. (2009). *Damage assessment for 5 PHCCs in Gaza Strip*. Technical Report. February. http://www.ochaopt.org/gazacrisis/infopool/opt_health_mdm_damage_assessment_5PHCCs_feb_2009.pdf

Coastal Municipalities Water Utility. (2009). *Damage assessment report: Water and waste water infrastructure and facilities, 27 December 2008-19 January 2009*. CMWU, Gaza.

Palestinian National Authority. (2009). *Damages report & recovery plan, solid waste management in Rafah*. Ministry of Local Government, Municipality of Rafah, Gaza. 27 March.

Office for Coordination of Humanitarian Affairs. (2009). *Gaza Flash Appeal*. Occupied Palestinian territories. OCHA, Gaza. http://www.ochaopt.org/documents/ocha_opt_handout_flash_appeal_english.pdf

World Health Organization. (2009). *Gaza Strip, Initial Health Needs Assessment*. WHO, Geneva. http://www.emro.who.int/Palestine/reports/monitoring/WHO_special_monitoring/gaza/Gaza%20Strip%20 Early%20Health%20Assessment%20(final)16Feb2009.pdf

Food and Agriculture Organization. (2009). *Gaza's farmers unable to recover from Operation Cast Lead*. FAO, Rome. http://unispal.un.org/unispal.nsf/db942872b9eae454852560f6005a76fb/6e287317a63ca2f a85257591004367888?OpenDocument

Food and Agriculture Organization. (2009). "Impact of Gaza crisis". *Agriculture Sector Report*. Palestine National Authority, Gaza. http://www.apis.ps/documents/AGR%20Sector%20Gaza%20Report_final.pdf

United Nations Children's Fund. (2009). *Initial field assessment: Water, Sanitation and Hygiene (WASH)*. UNICEF. http://www.ochaopt.org/gazacrisis/infopool/opt_wash_cluster_Initial_Field_Assessment_jan_2009.pdf

Coastal Municipalities Water Authority. (2009). *Israeli military offensive on Gaza fast track repairs and recovery plan report for water and waste water facilities, 20 January – 5 February 2009*. CMWA, Gaza.

Food and Agriculture Organization and World Food Programme. (2009). *Joint Emergency Food Security Assessment (EFSA): Gaza Strip main findings*. FAO and WFP, Jerusalem. http://www.apis.ps/documents/EFSA_donor_ppt_english-20090306.pdf

Office for the Coordination of Humanitarian Affairs. (2009). *List of all commitments/contributions and pledges as of 19 April 2009*. Occupied Palestinian territories. Compiled on the basis of information provided by donors and appealing organizations. OCHA, Geneva. http://www.reliefweb.int/fts: (Table ref: R10).

Paltel Group. (2009). *Losses and damage report of Paltel Group infrastructure*. Full losses and Damage report of Paltel Group's companies in Gaza strip due to Israeli war from 27 December 2008 to 18 January 2009. Gaza Directorate, Gaza.

UNDP/PAPP. (2009). *Public services and roads in Gaza Strip after the last 22 days of the war on Gaza*. UNDP. Jerusalem/Gaza. http://www.ochaopt.org/gazacrisis/infopool/opt_env_undp_Rubble_Circumstances_in_ Gaza_Strip_feb_2009.pdf

Office for Coordination of Humanitarian Affairs. (2009). *Rapid assessment summary*. OCHA, Geneva. http://www.ochaopt.org/gazacrisis/infopool/opt_wash_phg_Rapid_Assessment_Summary_jan_2009.pdf

Palestinian Hydrology Group. (2009). *Rapid community based water and sanitation needs assessment from the impact of the Israeli offensive on Gaza between 27 December 2008 and 17 January 2009.* Palestinian Hydrology Group, Ramallah.

UNDP/PAPP, Data SIO, NOAA, US NAVY,NGA, GEBCO. (2009). *Rapid livelihoods assessment for affected Areas in Gaza.* Post 27. Gaza City and Jerusalem.

Palestinian National Authority. (2009). *The Palestinian National Early Recovery and Reconstruction Plan for Gaza 2009-2010.* International Conference in Support of the Palestinian Economy for the Reconstruction of Gaza, Sharm El-Sheikh.

Office for Coordination of Humanitarian Affairs. (2009). *Summary table for damages in water and waste water facilities.* http://www.ochaopt.org/gazacrisis/infopool/opt_wash_cmwu_pwu_Preliminary_Damage_Assessment_jan_2009.pdf

SURGE work plan: Gaza early recovery. (2009). Prepared for UNDP/PAPP, Jerusalem.

The grave health situation caused by Israeli military operations in the occupied Palestinian territories, particularly in the occupied Gaza Strip. 124th Session EB124.R4, Agenda item 4.16, 21 January 2009. http://www.arableagueonline.org/las/picture_gallery/bayan21-1-2009en.pdf

Appendix III: References

Abu Naser, A.A., N. Ghbn, R. Khoudary. (2007). "Relation of nitrate contamination of groundwater with methaemoglobin level among infants in Gaza." *Eastern Mediterranean Health Journal*, 13(5):994-1004.

Al Absi, Awni A. (2008). *Nitrate contamination of ground water and Methemoglobinemia in Gaza Strip*. J. Al-Aqsa University, Gaza. http://www.alaqsa.edu.ps/ar/aqsamagazine/programing/twelve_edition/1.pdf

Al-Yaqubi, A., A. Alievi, Z. Mimi. (n.d.) *Domestic water demand management in terms of quality and quantity in Gaza Strip/Palestine*. Palestine Water Authority, Gaza.

Ashour, F., B. Ashour, M. Komarzynski, Y. Nassar, M. Kudla, N. Shawa, G. Henderson. (2009). *A brief outline of the sewage infrastructure and public health risks in the Gaza Strip for the World Health Organization*. EWASH.

Bolt, K., G. Ruta, M. Sarraf. (2005). *Estimating the cost of environmental degradation*. Training manual in English, French and Arabic. Paper No.106, Environment Department, World Bank, Washington, DC. September.

Brown, K., D. Pearce. (1994). 'The economic value of non-market benefits of tropical forests: Carbon storage." In J. Weiss (ed.), *The economics of project appraisal and the environment*. Edward Elgar Publishing Limited, Cheltenham.

Carson, R.T., R.C. Mitchell, M. Hanemann, R.J. Kopp, S. Presser, P. Ruud. (2004). Contingent valuation and cost of passive use: Damages from Exon Valdes oil spill. *Environmental and Resource Economics*, 25:257-286.

Coastal Municipalities Water Utility. (2009). *1st quarter report of waste water quality in the Gaza Strip for year 2009*. CMWU, Gaza.

Coastal Municipalities Water Utility. (2008). *Water situation in the Gaza Strip year 2007/2008*. CMWU, Gaza.

Cohen, M.J. (1995). "Technological disaster and natural resource damage assessment: An evaluation of the Exon Valdez oil spill." *Land Economics*, 71:65-82.

Dan, J., Y. Greitzer (1967). "The effect of soil landscape and quarternery geology on the distribution of saline and fresh water in the coastal plane of Israel." *Water Planning for Israel*, June 1967.

Dixon, J.A., M.M. Hufschmidt, (eds.). (1986). *Economic valuation techniques for the environment*. John Hopkins University Press, Baltimore and London.

Food and Agriculture Organization. (2009). "Impact of Gaza crisis". *Agriculture Sector Report*. Palestine National Authority, Gaza. http://www.apis.ps/documents/AGR%20Sector%20Gaza%20Report_final.pdf

Harrington, W., A. Krupnik, W. Spofford. (1989). "The economic losses of a waterborne disease outbreak." *Journal of Urban Economics*, 25(1):116-137.

Health and Safety Executive. (2005). *Health and Safety Guidelines*. HSE Books, U.K.

Lee, K., Y. Choi, C. Chae, and B. Jung, (2007). *The Estimation of the Energy Consumption and CO2 Emission at the Construction Stage*, Andong National University, Republic of Korea.

McCracken, J.R., H. Abaza. (2001). *Environmental valuation: A worldwide compendium of case studies*. Earthscan Pubications Ltd., London.

Environmental Assessment of the Gaza Strip

National Oceanic and Atmospheric Administration Panel. (1993). *Report of NOAA Panel on Contingent Valuation*. US Federal Register 58. NOAA, Washington, DC.

Palestinian National Authority. (2009). *The Palestine National Early Recovery and Reconstruction Plan for Gaza 2009-2010*. International Conference in Support of the Palestine Economy for the Reconstruction of Gaza, Sharm El-Sheikh.

Palestinian Water Authority. (2002). "Impact of the water crisis in the Gaza Strip". *Palestinian Water Authority Report*. Palestinian Water Authority, Gaza.

Ready, R., S. Navrud. (2006). "International benefit transfers: Methods and validity tests." *Ecological Economics*, 60:429-434.

Santhakumar, V., A. Chakraborty. (2003). "Environmental costs and their impact on the net present value of a hydro-electric project in Kerala, India." *Environment and Development Economics*, 8(2):311-338.

World Bank. (2007). *Economic assessment of environmental degradation due to July 2006 hostilities in the Republic of Lebanon – A Sector Note*. Report No. 39787-LB, Sustainable Development Department, Middle East and North Africa Region, World Bank, Washington, DC.

World Bank. (2002). *Arab Republic of Egypt: Cost assessment of environmental degradation*. Report No. 25175-EGT, World Bank, Washington, DC.

World Health Organization. (2009). *Gaza situation report*. WHO, Gaza.

World Health Organization. (2008). *Guidelines for drinking water quality; third edition, incorporating the first and second addenda. Volume 1: Recommendations*. WHO, Geneva.

World Health Organization. *Guidelines for safe recreational waters. Volume 1: Coastal and fresh waters*. WHO, Geneva.

Yaquibi, A. (2008). *Towards domestic groundwater supply management in the Gaza Strip governorates*. Palestine Water Authority, Gaza.

Zakout, H. (2007). *Groundwater level changes phenomena in the Gaza Strip*. Water Resource Directorate, Palestine National Authority, Gaza.

Appendix IV: Bibliography

1. Gray, A. (2007). *The water crisis in Gaza.* International View Point, News and Analysis from the fourth international; IV Online magazine: IV386-February. http://www.internationalviewpoint.org/spip.php?article1211

2. El-Fadel, M., M. Massoud. (2000). "Particulate matter in urban areas: A health-based economic assessment". *The Science of Total Environment,* 257:133-146.

3. World Bank. (2009). *Assessment of restrictions on Palestinian water sector development.* Report No. 47657-GZ, Sector Note, Sustainable Development Department, Middle East and North Africa Region, World Bank, Washington, DC.

4. Shomara, B., K. Osenbrückb, A. Yahyaa. (2008). *Elevated nitrate levels in the groundwater of the Gaza Strip: Distribution and sources.* Institute of Environmental Geochemistry, bUFZ – Helmholtz Centre for Environmental Research, Germany.

5. PALTRADE & Palestinian Federation of Industries in association with the Palestinian Private Sector Coordinating Council (PSCC). (2007). *Border closure "Effect on private sector in Gaza".* Gaza.

6. United Nations Environment Programme. (2009). *Common messaging on the flash appeal/CAP and early recovery.* UNEP, Geneva. http://unep-pcdmb.net/gaza/OPT%20April/CommonMessages%20-%20CAP%20-%20EarlyRecovery.pdf

7. Medecins Du Monde. (2009). *Damage assessment for 5 PHCCs in Gaza Strip* - Technical Report. France. http://www.ochaopt.org/gazacrisis/infopool/opt_health_mdm_damage_assessment_5PHCCs_feb_2009.pdf

8. Coastal Municipalities Water Utility. (2009). *Damage assessment report: Water and waste water infrastructure and facilities, 27 December 2008-19 January 2009.* CMWU, Gaza.

9. Palestinian National Authority. (2009). *Damages report & recovery plan, solid waste management in Rafah.* Ministry of Local Government, Municipality of Rafah, Gaza.

10. Sabatinelli, G. (2009). *Why an epidemiological bulletin for Gaza Strip?* Cover letter by UNRWA Director of Health.Amman, Jordan. http://ocha-gwapps1.unog.ch/rw/RWFiles2009.nsf/FilesByRWDocUnidFilename/MUMA-7SG4TW-full_report.pdf/$File/full_report.pdf

11. World Bank. (2007). *Economic assessment of environmental degradation due to July 2006 hostilities in the Republic of Lebanon – A Sector Note.* Report No. 39787-LB, Sustainable Development Department, Middle East and North Africa Region, World Bank, Washington, DC. 11 October.

12. United Nations Relief and Works Agency for Palestine. (2009). *Epidemiological Bulletin for Gaza Strip,* Volume 1, Issue 1. Department of Health, UNRWA. http://www.who.int/hac/crises/international/wbgs/gaza_unrwa_epi_15feb2009.pdf

13. United Nations Relief and Works Agency for Palestine. (2009). *Epidemiological Bulletin for Gaza Strip,* Volume 1, Issue 2. Department of Health, UNRWA. http://www.wwan.cn/unrwa/programmes/health/gaza_epidemiological_bulletin/issue2.pdf

14. Ashour, F., B. Ashour, M. Komarzynski, Y. Nassar, M. Kudla, N. Shawa, G. Henderson. (2009). *A brief outline of the sewage infrastructure and public health risks in the Gaza Strip for the World Health Organization.* EWASH. Gaza City, Jerusalem.

15. Office for the Coordination of Humanitarian Affairs. (2009). *Field update on Gaza from the humanitarian coordinator, situation overview*. OCHA, Geneva.

16. Office for the Coordination of Humanitarian Affairs. (2009). *Gaza Flash Appeal*. Occupied Palestinian Territory. OCHA, Geneva. http://www.ochaopt.org/documents/ocha_opt_handout_flash_appeal_english.pdf

17. World Health Organization. *Gaza Strip, Initial Health Needs Assessment*. (2009). WHO, Geneva. http://www.emro.who.int/Palestine/reports/monitoring/WHO_special_monitoring/gaza/Gaza%20Strip%20Early%20Health%20Assessment%20(final)16Feb2009.pdf

18. Food and Agriculture Organization. (2009). *Gaza's farmers unable to recover from Operation Cast Lead*. FAO, Rome. http://unispal.un.org/unispal.nsf/db942872b9eae454852560f6005a76fb/6e287317a63ca2fa8525759100436788?OpenDocument

19. Howard, G., J. Bartram. (2003). *Domestic water quantity, service level and health*. Water Engineering and Development Centre, Loughborough University, United Kingdom; Water, Sanitation and Health Programme, World Health Organization, Geneva. WHO/SDE/WSH/03.02. http://www.who.int/water_sanitation_healthdiseases/WHSH03.02.pdf

20. Baalousha, H. (2008). *Analysis of nitrate occurrence and distribution in groundwater in the Gaza strip using major Ion Chemistry*. Institute of Hydraulic Engineering and Water Resources Management, Faculty of Civil Engineering Aachen University of Technology (RWTH).

21. Baalousha, H. (2005.) "Desalination status in the Gaza Strip and its environmental impact." Institute of Hydraulic Engineering and Water Resources Management, Aachen University of Technology. *Desalination*, 196(2006):1-12.

22. Food and Agriculture Organization. (2009). "Impact of Gaza Crisis". *Agriculture Sector Report*. Palestine National Authority, Gaza. http://www.apis.ps/documents/AGR%20Sector%20Gaza%20Report_final.pdf

23. United Nations Children's Fund. (2009). *Initial field assessment: Water, Sanitation and Hygiene (WASH)*. UNICEF, Geneva. http://www.ochaopt.org/gazacrisis/infopool/opt_wash_cluster_Initial_Field_Assessment_jan_2009.pdf

24. Coastal Municipalities Water Authority. (2009). *Israeli military offensive on Gaza fast track repairs and recovery plan report for water and waste water facilities, 20 January-5 February 2009*. CMWA, Gaza.

25. Tiedje, J.M.(1988). "Ecology of denitrification and dissimilatory nitrate reduction to ammonium." *Biology of anaerobic microorganisms*. Lisbon. http://biomicro.sdstate.edu/GibsonS/pdf_folder/nitrate.pdf

26. Food and Agriculture Organization and World Food Programme. (2009). *Joint Emergency Food Security Assessment (EFSA): Gaza Strip main findings*. FAO and WFP, Jerusalem.

27. Bolt, Katherine, Giovanni Ruta, Maria Sarraf. (2005). *Estimating the cost of environmental degradation*. Training manual in English, French and Arabic. Paper No. 106, Environment Department, World Bank, Washington, DC.

28. Office for the Coordination of Humanitarian Affairs. (2009). *List of all commitments/contributions and pledges as of 19 April 2009*. Occupied Palestinian territories. Compiled on the basis of information provided by donors and appealing organizations. OCHA, Geneva. http://www.reliefweb.int/fts: (Table ref: R10).

29. Paltel Group. (2009). *Full losses and Damage report of Paltel Group's companies in Gaza strip due to Israeli war from 27 December 2008 to 18 January 2009*. Gaza Directorate, Gaza.

30. Almasri, M. N., S. Ghabayen, J. J. Kaluarachchi, A. Jarrar, A. J. M. McKee. (2005). *A conceptual framework for managing nitrate contamination of the Gaza coastal aquifer, Palestine.* Impacts of Global Climate Change, World Water and Environmental Resources Congress 2005, Anchorage, Alaska. http://blogs.najah.edu/staff/emp_3037/article/A-Conceptual-Framework-for-Managing-Nitrate-Contamination-of-the-Gaza-Coastal-Aquifer-Palestine

31. Al-Agha, M. R. (1997). "Environmental management in the Gaza Strip". *Environment Impact Assessment Review*, 17:65-76. The Islamic University of Gaza, Elsevier Science Inc.

32. UNDP/PAPP. (2009). *Public buildings: Overall summary.* 9 February 2009.

33. UNDP/PAPP. (2009). *Public services and roads in Gaza Strip after the last 22 days of the war on Gaza.* UNDP/PAPP, Jerusalem. http://www.ochaopt.org/gazacrisis/infopool/opt_env_undp_Rubble_Circumstances_in_Gaza_Strip_feb_2009.pdf

34. Palestinian Hydrology Group. (2009). *Rapid community based water and sanitation needs assessment from the impact of the Israeli offensive on Gaza between 27 December 2008 and 17 January 2009.* Palestinian Hydrology Group, Ramallah.

35. UNDP/PAPP, Data SIO, NOAA, US NAVY, NGA, GEBCO. (2008). *Rapid livelihoods assessment for affected areas in Gaza.* Post 27 December. Gaza city and Jerusalem.

36. UNEP. (2009). *Lab results.* Bachema AG Analytical Laboratories, Schlieren, Switzerland. Post-Conflict and Disaster Management Branch, UNEP, Geneva.

37. Sarhan, S. (2009). *Occupied Palestinian territories: Gaza Flash Appeal.* http://www.unfpa.org/emergencies/gaza/docs/gaza_flash_appeal.pdf

38. Palestinian National Authority. (2009). *The Palestinian National Early Recovery and Reconstruction Plan for Gaza 2009-2010.* International Conference in Support of the Palestinian Economy for the Reconstruction of Gaza, Sharm Al Sheikh.

39. Palestinian National Authority. (2009). *Conclusions by the chair.* International Conference in Support of the Palestinian Economy for the Reconstruction of Gaza, Sharm El-Sheikh. http://unispal.un.org/unispal.nsf/bc8b0c56b7bf621185256cbf005ac05f/3f64338e11ed7eac8525756e004fda82?OpenDocument

40. OAS,UNEP & IETC. (1997). *Source book of alternative technologies for freshwater augmentation in Latin America and the Caribbean. 2.1 Desalination by reverse osmosis.* Washington, U.S.A. http://www.oas.org/dsd/publications/Unit/oea59e/ch20.htm

41. Office for Coordination of Humanitarian Affairs. (2009). *Summary table for damages in water and waste water facilities.* OCHA, Geneva. http://www.ochaopt.org/gazacrisis/infopool/opt_wash_cmwu_pwu_Preliminary_Damage_Assessment_jan_2009.pdf

42. *SURGE work plan – Gaza early recovery.* (2009). Prepared for UNDP/PAPP, Jerusalem.

43. *The grave health situation caused by Israeli military operations in the occupied Palestinian territories, particularly in the occupied Gaza Strip.* 124th Session EB124.R4, Agenda item 4.16, 21 January 2009. http://www.arableagueonline.org/las/picture_gallery/bayan21-1-2009en.pdf

44. The Portland Trust. (2008). *Palestinian Economic Bulletin*, Issue 27. http://www.portlandtrust.org/Bulletin%20Issue%2027%20December%202008.pdf

45. The Portland Trust. (2009). *Palestinian Economic Bulletin*, Issue 28.
    http://www.portlandtrust.org/Bulletin%20Issue%2028%20January%202009.pdf

46. The Portland Trust. (2009). *Palestinian Economic Bulletin*, Issue 29.
    http://www.portlandtrust.org/Bulletin%20Issue%2029%20February%202009.pdf

47. United Nations Environment Programme. (2009). *Comment on the analytical results.* Bachema AG
    Analytical Laboratories, 20090894, Schlieren, Switzerland. UNEP, Geneva.

48. Frenkel, V., T. Gourgi. (1994). *Brackish water RO desalination plant in the Gaza Strip.* Desalination 101
    (1995) 47-50, Electrical Mechanical Services (EMS), subsidiary of Mekoroth Water Company Israel.

49. Sanjour, W. (1975). *Policy implications of sewage sludge on hazardous waste regulation.* Office of
    Solid Waste Management Programs, United States Environmental Protection Agency, Washington, DC.
    http://pwp.lincs.net/sanjour/Sludge1.htm

50. Sattout, E., S. Talhouk, P. Caligari. (2007). "Economic value of cedar relics in Lebanon: An application
    of contingent valuation method for conservation." *Ecological Economics*, 61(2-3):315-322.

51. Abu Naser, A.A. (2003). *Relationship between nitrate contamination of groundwater and methemoglobin
    level among infants in Jabalia, Gaza and Khanyounis.* School of Public Health, Al Quds University,
    Jerusalem.

52. Health and Safety Executive. (2005). *Health and Safety Guidelines.* HSE Books, U.K.

Appendix V: List of contributors

Gaza Assessment Team

Muralee Thummarukudy, Post-Conflict and Disaster Management Branch, UNEP (Team Leader)
Joanne Stutz, Post-Conflict and Disaster Management Branch, UNEP
Firas Abu Taeh, Post-Conflict and Disaster Management Branch, UNEP
Mario Burger, Spiez Laboratory, Switzerland
Olof Linden, World Maritime University, Sweden
Thorsten Kallnischkies, Independent Consultant, Germany
David Smith, AH Allen Limited, United Kingdom
Santhakumar Velappan Nair, Center for Development Studies, India

UN Early Recovery Assessment / Environment

Michael J. Cowing, Post Conflict and Disaster Management Branch, UNEP

Regional Office for Western Asia

Habib El Habr, Director and Regional Representative, UNEP

Regional Office for Europe

Christophe Bouvier, Director and Regional Representative, UNEP

Background Support

Yves Barthélemy, GIS Consultant, France
Sandhya Sreekumar, Research Associate, India

Laboratory Analysis

A.H. Allen Ltd., United Kingdom
Bachema AG Analytical Laboratory, Switzerland
Carbotech Laboratory, Switzerland
GBA Fruit Analytic GMBH, Sweden

Editors

Jane Upperton, United Kingdom
AvisAnne Julien, France

Photographs

Thaer M. Al-Hassani, Gaza

Thematic and Logistics Support

UNDP (Jerusalem and Gaza)

Khaled Shahwan. Deputy Special Representative (Operations)
Rima Abu- Middain Barghothi. Team Leader - Environment and Natural Capital
Ruba El-Ghoul. General Services Officer
Suzanne Abboud. Administrative Assistant-Travel Unit
Ahmad Al Reyati, Senior Project Engineer
Rezeq Awd, Site Engineer
Jehad Al Khatib, Project Manager
Hala Othman, Project Manager

UNDSS (Jerusalem and Gaza)

Savita Hande. Chief Security Advisor and Head of UNDSS in Jerusalem, West Bank, and Gaza
Andrew Pollock. Field Security Co-ordination Officer Gaza
Peggy Wheller. Field Security Adviser
Ahmad Al-Wazir. National Security Officer

WHO (Gaza)

Mahmood Daher, National Health Officer

UNRWA (Gaza)

Abdul-Karim Jouda. Chief - Environmental, Health Programme

UNOSAT

Frederic Lemoine
Luca Dell Oro
Ana Gago Da Silva
Josh Lyons

UNEP Post-Conflict and Disaster Management Branch (Geneva)

Henrik Slotte, Chief of Branch
Asif Ali Zaidi, Operations Manager
David Jensen, Policy and Planning Coordinator
Andrew Morton, Programme Manager, DR Congo and Haiti
Muralee Thummarukudy, Project Coordinator
Andrew Tomita, Research Assistant
Anne-Cécile Vialle, Associate Programme Officer
Altan Butt, Operations Assistant
Catherine Sullivan, Project Advisor
Dawit Yared, Project Assistant
Elena Orlyk, Project Assistant
Hannah Moosa, Research Assistant
Hannoa Guillaume-Davin, Project Advisor
Hassan Partow, Programme Officer
Joanne Stutz, Programme Assistant
Julien Aguzzoli, Research Assistant
Kenneth Chulley, Technical Assistant
Lucile Gingembre, Associate Programme Officer
Maliza van Eeden, Project Coordinator
Mani Nair, Administrative and Financial Assistant
Mario Burger, Senior Scientific Advisor
Marisol Estrella, Programme Officer
Matija Potocnik, Media Assistant
Matthias Chesley, Research Assistant
Maximilien Pardo y Fernandez, Associate Programme Officer
Michael J. Cowing, Project Coordinator
Nita Venturelli, Financial Assistant
Peter Dugbaek, Associate Programme Officer
Renard Sexton, Project Advisor
Reshmi Thakur, Communications Assistant
Sarah Bieber, Research Assistant
Satu Ojaluoma, Administrative Officer
Silja Halle, Communications Advisor
Zuzana Burivalova, Intern